CLIMBS ON ALPINE PEAKS

BENN'S ESSEX LIBRARY
Edited by Edward G. Hawke, M.A.

Abate Achille Ratti

(POPE PIUS XI)

CLIMBS ON ALPINE PEAKS

*Translated by J. E. C. EATON
With a Foreword by DOUGLAS
FRESHFIELD, and an Introduction
by the
Right Rev. L. C. CASARTELLI,
Bishop of Salford*

LONDON: ERNEST BENN LTD.
Bouverie House, Fleet Street.

The Publishers desire to acknowledge
the courtesy of the Italian Alpine Club
for the use of the articles that have
appeared in the "Rivista" and "Bollettino" of that Club.

First Published 1923
Second Impression 1925
Third Impression (Essex Library) ... 1929

INTRODUCTION

THE Publishers of this most interesting volume—equally interesting for its subject-matter and for the personality of the author—have done me the honour of asking me to write a few words of introduction. "Good wine needs no bush," and, in any case, I feel that I have no particular qualifications to undertake such a task, particularly after the illuminating Foreword of so eminent an Alpinist as Mr. Douglas Freshfield. For I am not an Alpinist in any sense of the word —though I do look back to a delightful holiday at the Schwarzsee and the Hörnli, referred to by the illustrious author of the following essays. Perhaps the only claim I have to speak at all is that I was, as I believe, the first to translate into English from an Italian review some extracts from the description of his climbs by the then Abate Ratti, which were reprinted in 1921 when he was

made Archbishop of Milan. The writer
I have had the privilege to know person-
ally since his visit to Manchester in 1900
and subsequently at the splendid Biblioteca Ambrosiana of Milan, that noble
creation of the illustrious Cardinal
Federigo Borromeo, so familiar to readers
of Manzoni's immortal *Promessi Sposi*.
For if Don Achille Ratti was in the front
rank of Alpine climbers, none the less
was he in the front rank of librarians,
whether in his beloved Ambrosiana, or,
subsequently, in the Vatican Library.

However, I have been asked to say
a few words on the biography of the first
Alpinist Pope, though I think the remarkable career of Pius XI. is pretty
well known through many articles in
the Press. It has been my good fortune
to spend many happy days in the small,
busy manufacturing town (or large village, if you prefer) of Desio, a few miles
outside of Milan, with its fine domed
parish church and its busy silk weaving
and dyeing works. In this little town
on March 31, 1857, was born Achille

Ratti, whose father was connected with one of the great silk concerns just referred to. His earliest education he owed to an uncle, a pious and learned priest, to whom he has always referred with sentiments of veneration and gratitude. Early called to the ecclesiastical state, he continued his studies, first in the Seminary of his native diocese and subsequently in the Lombard College of Rome, greatly distinguishing himself and taking high degrees. He was ordained priest in 1879, and said his first Mass in the Lombard Church of San Carlo in Corso, and then returned to begin his priestly career in Milan. For many subsequent years of strenuous labour he lived a life which may be described as one of triple activities, carried on with almost passionate enthusiasm : that of the scholar, a profound and brilliant cultivator of historical and palæographical sciences, and particularly an enlightened and indefatigable librarian ; that of the intrepid and yet thoroughly scientific Alpinist, as revealed in the subsequent pages ; that of the pious and earnest pastor of souls, particularly devoted to the spiritual care of the young, including the poorest children of the great city, under the care of the good religious of the " Cenacolo," which he served as chaplain for over thirty years.

In the Library he was at first assistant to the eminent Orientalist, Ceriani, whom he eventually succeeded as Prefect. As such, he entirely reorganised that invaluable treasure-house of books and works of art. I shall not touch upon his many publications on various subjects of history and palæography, because they are fully treated by the writer of the first chapter of this book. (The late Benedict XV., when creating Mgr. Ratti a Cardinal in 1921, after his return from his diplomatic mission, with a gentle humour almost worthy of his predecessor the fourteenth of that name, referred to his eminence as a " diplomatico," in the double sense of the Italian word—our " diplomatist " and an archival scholar.) His brilliant work in the Ambrosian led to the Pope calling him to Rome to the famous Vatican Library, where he at first worked under Cardinal Gasquet, and then under Father Ehrle, S.J. (since created by him Cardinal), and eventually as himself head of the Library. If Rome and its Library put an end to his Alpine climbing, his sudden transfer by Benedict XV. in 1918 to diplomacy, as Apostolic Visitor and afterwards Nuncio to Poland, put an end to his career as Librarian. Three years later he was recalled by the same Pontiff from his brilliantly successful diplomatic career to undertake the pastoral charge of his native diocese, that of Milan, one of the largest in the world, with over two million souls, in succession to the late saintly Cardinal Ferrari, and simultaneously was created Cardinal, June 13, 1921.

The rest is known. Within seven months Pope Benedict was carried off after a few days' illness, and not many days later, on February 6, 1922, Achille Ratti was elected Pope by the Conclave and took the name of Pius XI.

His elevation to the Papacy has not destroyed his love of Alpinism, though it has for ever cut him off from its pursuit. Nothing has given him greater pleasure than the courteous greeting from the Mount Everest Expedition. And when he lately received the handsome illustrated report of that famous deed of mountaineering, he sat up quite late at night reading it. The Himalayan climbers also had the graceful idea of sending to His Holiness a fragment of rock broken from the highest point which they reached, handsomely mounted in silver, with the names of all the expedition engraved on a plate, and enclosed in a mahogany case. This memento Pius XI. greatly values—a photograph of it lies before me as I write.

Louis Charles,
Bishop of Salford

ROME,
    January 30, 1923.

FOREWORD

THOSE who, like the present writer, can look back as far as the middle of the last century easily recognise various and very marked stages in the growth of mountaineering adventure. Up to that date the portion of our globe above the snow-line, the white islands that diversify the temperate and even the tropical zones, had, like the Polar wastes, been regarded as forbidden ground, only to be trespassed on by daring adventurers, and then at their imminent peril. The worthy Bishops and Abbots who were forced to intrude on the Alps in order to reach the goal of their pilgrimage, Rome, looked on the Great St. Bernard, the Mons Jovis, as the haunt of a Pennine army of evil spirits, " Penninus exercitus malignorum spirituum."

In the middle of the eighteenth century

Rousseau's enthusiasm and eloquence first called men's attention to the Swiss lowlands, the flowery pastures and orchards of Canton Vaud. A few years later De Saussure's scientific explorations and mountain climbs drew public attention to the beauties as well as the terrors of the snows, and started the procession of " Visitors to the Glaciers " which disturbed Gibbon at Lausanne. To their leaders, the pioneers of Alpine exploration in the eighteenth century, the Church contributed largely. The Benedictine monk of Disentis, Placidus à Spescha (1752 to 1833), climbed vigorously and successfully among the mountains of Graubünden, and, as Mr. Coolidge has justly remarked, must always be bracketed with De Saussure in the annals of mountaineering. In the same century we find one of the Canons of the Great St. Bernard, M. Murith, scaling Mont Vélan, and M. Clément, the Curé of Val d'Illiez, conquering the Dent du Midi.

Swiss scientists had about 1840 been already at work among the glaciers of the Bernese Oberland. But it was the birth of the Alpine Club in 1857 which marked an epoch, the beginning throughout Western Europe of a new and popular form of nature-worship. The Alps were for the first time recognised—in Leslie Stephen's phrase—as a playground. Their appeal was discovered to be many-sided ; to some it came mainly as a challenge to a new form of exercise and sport ; to some as a means for physical research, or for intellectual enjoyment of the marvels of nature ; while to not a few " the deep and, as it were, religious silence of the highest crests " afforded, as to Conrad Gesner in the sixteenth century, those rare intervals of spiritual vision in which the riddle of the universe seems for a moment less beyond the reach of our mortal intellects.

Each nation of Western Europe—Italy, urged by her statesman Quintino Sella, among the first—made haste to found its climbing fraternity, and several of these soon counted their members by thousands. The new cult, no doubt, had extravagances which provoked the ready criticism of those whom bodily or mental indisposition hindered from taking part in it; and this criticism found an eloquent exponent in a great writer and lover of mountains, John Ruskin. Vigorous youths, he delighted to point out, made mountaineering a cover for acrobatic performances of a highly dangerous and objectionable character; they "treated the Alps as greased poles." But the impartial public applauded and passed on, recognising that those who came to climb, as a rule, soon succumbed to the influence of the Cathedrals of Nature and remained to worship. The great mountains were generally recognised, not only as a place of recovery for men's bodies, but also of rest and refreshment for their souls.

In the modern developments of Alpine travel, as in its origins, the Church has played a conspicuous part. The Gross Glockner was conquered as early as 1800 by a party organised by Cardinal Count Franz von Salm, Prince-Bishop of Gurk, who himself, though unsuccessfully, joined in the expedition. About 1840 a Prince-Archbishop of Prague (previously of Salzburg), who was also a Cardinal, made three new ascents in the same group. Other ecclesiastics who took a leading share in Tyrolese climbing were Peter Karl Thurwieser and Valentin Stanig.

More names might doubtless be added from the Western Alps. Two of the peaks of Monte Rosa itself, those subsequently known as the Vincent Pyramide and the Signal Kuppe, were climbed by the parish priests of Gressoney and Alagna respectively. Coming to my own day, I have pleasant recollections of meetings, as a boy, with Chanoine Carrel, who did so much for his native Val d' Aosta and Cogne, with Pfarrer Imseng of Saas, Sir Alfred Wills' friend, and at a later date with that active mountaineer Herr Senn, of Fend, in the Œtzthal. But none of these clerical precursors equalled, or in any way approached, the feats so vividly recorded in the following pages. These are of a

character that firmly establishes the claim
of Pope Pius XI. to a place in the front
rank of mountaineers. But before I deal
with them more in detail, English readers
may welcome a brief sketch of the leading
points in the life of His Holiness.

Achille Ratti was born in 1857, the
son of well-to-do parents resident in the
small town of Desio, situated in the
Lombard plain, a little north of Monza
and between Milan and Como, in full
view, therefore, of the snowy crest of
Monte Rosa. His father was the manager
of a silk factory in his native place. The
future Pope was one of a family of seven;
he had five brothers, of whom only one
is now living, and a sister. The surviving
brother, Carlo Ratti, has been an active
climber, and was Editor for seventeen
years of the publications of the Italian
Alpine Club. He was among the explorers of the Val Masino district, the
fascinating group of grey granite peaks
that look down both on St. Moritz and
on the Lago di Como, and one of its
minor summits has been named after him.

Achille Ratti went as a boy to school at Desio, but his summer holidays were spent with a clerical uncle at Asso, an upland village hidden away in the green heart of the Bellagio promontory, and sheltered by chestnut groves and lawns that command marvellous views over the upper reaches of Lago di Como. Here the lad's character and ability attracted the notice of the then Archbishop of Milan, and he was consequently sent to be educated at the Theological Seminary in that city, whence he went in due course to the Collegio Lombardo at Rome. Having completed a distinguished career by obtaining at the Gregorian University the triple Doctorate in Philosophy, Theology, and Canon Law, he was at the age of twenty-two ordained Priest, and, after a three years' interval, returned to Milan as a Professor in the Theological Seminary.

Five years later Mgr. Ratti was appointed Subdirector of the great Ambrosian Library, where he worked for twenty-three years, succeeding in 1907 to the higher post. " It would be impossible," writes Cardinal Gasquet, "to speak in detail of the contributions to Italian literature and history which proceeded from the pen of Mgr. Ratti during this period. He became known and honoured for the courteous and ever-ready welcome he gave to all students who consulted the famous library, and for the way in which he placed at their disposal his knowledge and advice."

Mgr. Ratti's duties in the library, his researches among its codices and incunabula, and his own extensive literary activities, did not hinder him from finding time for the work of a zealous priest. He assisted a community of nuns, of which he was the chaplain, in their social and charitable endeavours. But his special pleasure was in the instruction of the young. "It was," writes a colleague, "a spectacle which gave edification to many to see the learned Prefect of the Ambrosian Library spending the afternoons of feast days in teaching Catechism to the ragged little urchins (mostly chimney-sweeps) whom he brought together from all parts into the church of S. Sepolcro."

In 1910 Mgr. Ratti was called to Rome to assist the Prefect of the Vatican Library, and four years later succeeded to the chief post. Here, without allowing his own literary and critical labours to suffer any interruption, he showed in every direction his immense energy in administrative work. The best proof of the impression made by Mgr. Ratti on those he came most in contact with was given when, in 1918, this congenial employment was interrupted by his being sent, first as Apostolic Visitor and afterwards as Nuncio, to Poland and eventually to Russia, to look after the interests of the Church in the changes consequent on the world crisis. In this very difficult position Mgr. Ratti showed the strength of his character, as well as his political tact and powers of conciliation. When Warsaw was threatened by the Bolshevists he alone among the Foreign Ministers refused to leave the city.

On his return to Rome in 1921 Mgr.

Ratti was created a Cardinal and Archbishop of Milan, and in February, 1922,
he was elected Pope, a choice which
proved a welcome surprise not only to
the Catholic world, but to scholars and
men of learning throughout Europe.

It should be added that His Holiness
has been more than once in England,
and has studied among the MSS. of the
British Museum and the Bodleian at
Oxford. The following chapters prove
that he has also as intimate an acquaintance with the contemporary Alpine literature of this country as with the
palimpsests of the Ambrosian Library.
That he has not, as Pope, lost his warm
interest in the annals of mountain adventure, the message he was good enough
to send recently to our explorers on
Mount Everest affords a convincing proof:
" May God, who dwells on the heights,
bless the expedition."

From this outline of a distinguished
career I turn to the main purpose of this
note, to call attention to the place Alpine
climbing has held among Pope Pius XI.'s

many activities. His own accounts of his climbs (here translated by Mr. Eaton from his contributions to the publications of the Italian Alpine Club) form an essential contribution to the study of a remarkable character. They show that this learned young bookman and devoted priest was also a bold mountaineer, animated with a keen love of adventure, and endowed with high courage and unlimited powers of endurance. The story of Mgr. Ratti's career as a climber indicates a very natural preference for Italian mountains. In an ascent of the Grand Paradis, the highest peak wholly in Italy, he met with an adventure, not mentioned in this volume, which has been thus recorded by his companion: "On the glacier our guide fell into a crevasse, and would have perished had it not been for the presence of mind, skill, and strength with which Ratti held the rope and little by little succeeded in drawing him back to safety."

Let me take next, as an example of Mgr. Ratti's energy and endurance, the crossing of Monte Rosa, of which an account follows. Few more daring feats are on record. The ascent of the precipitous face of Monte Rosa above Macugnaga was for years reckoned one of the unsolved problems of the Alps. It was accomplished at last and more than once, but not by Italians. The successful climbers on their return agreed in declaring that, owing to the unavoidable risk incurred from avalanches and falling stones, the expedition ought to be banned.

Mgr. Ratti's patriotism made him eager that this spectacular feat should be repeated by his countrymen ; but at the same time he recognised that for responsible climbers a moral dilemma lay behind its physical difficulties. He is careful to tell his readers how ingeniously he overcame the former. By a prolonged preliminary study of the mountain he convinced himself that there were brief periods when loose stones were at rest and avalanches ceased from falling, and that by taking advantage of one of these intervals the climb might be attempted without any undue risk. And, after its accomplishment, he found himself able to assure the Alpine public that he and his companions—the party consisted of himself, a colleague, Professor Grasselli, and two Courmayeur guides—met with no perils with which they did not find themselves competent to cope. In short, he applied to the particular case in question the generally sound maxim that there are no such things as safe and dangerous mountains, but that every mountain has its good and bad moments.

The climb as described was, however, if not dangerous—and I would not venture to argue with so sound a mountaineer—arduous to the last degree. Starting from a hut at the height of 10,500 feet, the climbers took eighteen hours to conquer the precipices of the eastern face of the mountain and gain the Ost Spitze, a point on the spur of the Allerhöchste or Dufour Spitze, but close to its junction with the Alpine watershed. Finding, at 7.30 p.m., that it was too late to traverse the ridge connecting the two points, they descended a hundred feet and passed the night on a rocky ledge at a height of 15,000 feet. Next morning they completed the ascent of the Dufour Spitze, returned to their bivouac on the Italian slope of the mountain, and then forced the first passage of the Zumstein Sattel, the gap in the watershed between the junction of the Dufour Spitze spur and the Zumstein Spitze, finally descending by the Grenz Glacier to be benighted under the rocks of the Gornergrat. These were two prodigious days, while to sleep out without wraps or shelter at the height at which they spent their first night was an adventure few would care to imitate. Yet Mgr. Ratti and his hardy companions did not suffer to a degree that prevented them from enjoying the silence of the stars and the glory of the sunrise seen from their lofty perch. Professor Grasselli, it is true, had his hands frost-bitten, but this came from having to handle the rocks after unfortunately losing his ice-axe.

A week later we find Mgr. Ratti

starting with three guides to climb the Matterhorn *in the day* from Zermatt, and —the conditions being not altogether favourable—forced in the descent to spend a night on the rocks below the Shoulder. This experience he describes as thoroughly enjoyable !

Next year it was the turn of Mont Blanc. The summit was gained by the ordinary Courmayeur route, the party condescending to sleep in the Sella and Vallot huts. A descent, apparently in part at least new, was effected without difficulty by the western branch of the Glacier du Dôme and the Miage Glacier.

In a concluding chapter Mgr. Ratti relates how his favourite guide, Gadin of Courmayeur, and a Milanese nobleman were badly frost-bitten, and nearly lost their lives in forcing a passage across the Bergamasque Alps from Val Seriana to the Val Tellina in early spring over snowy wastes, where — *experto crede* — three months later the rare wanderer from beaten tracks finds himself in a glorious garden of gentians and rare primulas.

English mountaineers must feel greatly indebted to His Holiness for allowing them to read these spirited accounts of his daring and successful climbs of thirty years ago. They show in every page the kindliness and humour of the man, as well as the technical skill and judgment of the true mountaineer. They bear eloquent witness to his passion for the heights and the glories they reveal. Most of his readers will lay down the book with the hope that the course of Italian politics may allow Pope Pius XI. to live to enjoy once more the sunrise on the crest he conquered so gallantly. The snows of Soracte viewed from the windows of the Vatican can be but a poor substitute for the vision of Monte Rosa shining "faintly flushed and phantom-fair" among the spires of his former cathedral.

Douglas W. Freshfield

TRANSLATOR'S PREFACE

THE election of Cardinal Achille Ratti to the Papacy, as Pope Pius XI., awakened the greatest interest among mountaineers all over the world, for the new Pope was well known as a most distinguished and enthusiastic climber.

This book contains the Pope's description of various expeditions, the traverses of Monte Rosa and Mont Blanc in particular being of such a nature that any mountaineer might justly be proud of them.

The narrative is simple and charming, and every line of it indicates true love of the mountains, displays daring combined with prudence, and gives proof of kindness of heart and unfailing consideration for others.

Soon after Cardinal Ratti's elevation to the Holy See it occurred to Mr. Fisher

Unwin that the occasion would prove most suitable for endeavouring to collect the Pope's various Alpine writings and for publishing them in a book.

Mr. Unwin accordingly requested me to undertake the translation, and I have done the work to the best of my ability.

If the translation should appear to be too literal in places, let it be remembered that it was necessary for me to bear in mind above all the Italian saying *Traduttore traditore*, and that a literal translation helps, at any rate, to lessen, if it does not eliminate, the danger of losing or misrepresenting the various shades of meaning in the original.

CONTENTS

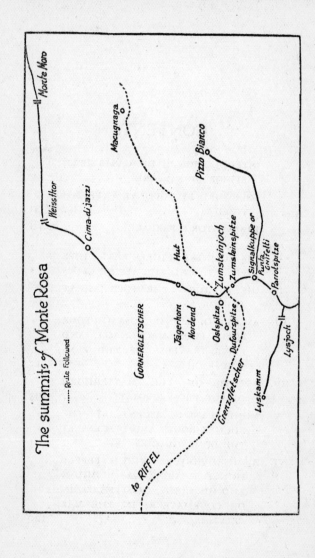

The summits of Monte Rosa

...... Route Followed

Monte Moro

Weiss-Thor

Cima-di-Jazzi

Macugnaga

Pizzo Bianco

Hut

Zumsteinjoch

Zumsteinspitze

Signalkuppe or
Punta
Gnifetti

Parrodspitze

GORNERGLETSCHER

Jägerhorn
Nordend

Ostspitze

Dufourspitze

Grenzgletscher

Lyskamm

Lysjoch

to RIFFEL

CHAPTER ONE

HIS HOLINESS ACHILLE RATTI, POPE PIUS XI., AND THE ALPINE CLUBS *

THE election of Achille Ratti to the Papacy has been an occasion for universal rejoicing, not only in Italy, but all over the world, and has been greeted with special joy by the Italian Alpine Club, which looks upon the triumph of its member, that great and valiant mountaineer, as almost a happy and glorious family event.

The President, as soon as he received the news, knowing that he would thus correctly interpret the wishes and inmost feelings of the members, hastened to express his personal delight to His Holiness in the following telegram :

" The Italian Alpine Club is justly

*From the *Rivista Mensile* of the Italian Alpine Club for January and February, 1922, vol. xli., Nos. 1 and 2.

proud, touched and happy that Achille Ratti, its esteemed and beloved honorary member, valiant mountaineer, enthusiastic admirer of the supreme beauties of the mountains and of their sublime influence on the temper of man's body and mind, in enabling him to face successfully the perils of life, learned of the learned, best of the good, has, during his ascent from earth to heaven, the greatest vouchsafed to any mortal, been elevated, by God's goodwill, to the supreme dignity of the Papacy. The Club sends him the assurance of its admiration, devotion and affection, and draws from the event the happiest and dearest auguries for the welfare of religion and the mother country of Italy."

This reverent and affectionate message from the Club proved most grateful to His Holiness Achille Ratti, as is shown by the following reply to the President :

" The new Pope is highly gratified at the noble message of congratulation on his election which you have so kindly sent in the name of the Italian Alpine Club, assures you of his affectionate thanks, and rejoices that he can, amid the heavy burdens of his office, point to the ennobling

efforts of the mountaineer as a true means
to uplift the spirit of mankind, and to
bring it nearer to God in the contem-
plation of the eternal beauties of the
mountains.

"CARDINAL GASPARRI."

"May our august member, who has
ever preferred and loved the beauties of
the mountains above all others that are
visible and tangible; who, by his bold
climbs on Monte Rosa, Mont Blanc and
the Matterhorn, 'imparted a new direction to Italian mountaineering, and
showed the way to its latter deeds of
daring, yet ever sounded a warning against
foolhardiness in risking life;' who even
now points from his high seat to the noble
efforts of the mountaineer as a sure means
to uplift the spirit of mankind; may our
august member, His Holiness Achille
Ratti, watch as it were like a guardian and
propitiatory spirit over the bold under-
takings and the glorious future of our
beloved Club.

"(*Signed*) B. CALDERINI,

"*President*."

The Alpine Club, London, has also

expressed to His Holiness Pius XI. its satisfaction at his elevation to the supreme dignity of the Papacy, in a telegram to which His Holiness deigned to send a reply.

Copy of telegram sent to His Holiness the Pope, February 8th, 1922 :

" The Alpine Club, London, rejoices at the election of so distinguished a mountaineer to the Papacy, and sends its most sincere and respectful congratulations."

Copy of telegram received February 12th, 1922 :

" PRESIDENT ALPINE CLUB, LONDON.

" The Holy Father thanks you for your devoted message, and sends you his blessing.

" (*Signed*) CARDINAL GASPARRI."

That famous mountaineer Captain J. P. Farrar, the editor of the *Alpine Journal*, forwarded copies of the two telegrams to our colleague G. Bobba, honorary

member of the Alpine Club, and enclosed
with them the following letter :

"MY DEAR FRIEND,

"I enclose a copy of a telegram which
we ventured to send to Monsignor Ratti,
and one of the reply with which he honoured us.   We are overjoyed that so true
and distinguished a mountaineer has been
raised to the papal throne.

"Sincere greetings from your affectionate friend.

"(*Signed*) J. P. F."

CHAPTER TWO

HIS HOLINESS THE POPE AS AN AUTHOR*

THE new Pope is stated in some London newspapers to have "written 330 books, great and small"; but many of the so-called "small" are tiny tracts of eight or twelve pages, which cannot by any stretch of imagination be called "books." Pius XI. (formerly Cardinal Achille Ratti) has been certainly a prolific writer, and, besides "real" books, a list of his contributions to periodical publications and transactions of learned societies would occupy about six columns of this journal. There has been also some confusion in the London dailies and weeklies with regard to his

* This chapter is reprinted from the *Publishers' Circular* for March, 1922, by permission of its author, Mr. A. de Ternant.

published reminiscences of mountaineering. He has certainly given to the world of sport some interesting papers on the subject, but the majority attributed to him belong in reality to his relative, Carlo Ratti, part-editor of the *Rivista Alpina Italiana*, and an energetic organiser of excursions. The present Pope, when a small boy, first heard the English language spoken on the Alps, and the party consisted of a Church of England clergyman and his family. Achille Ratti was immediately fascinated with the sound of the strange language, so different from Latin and his own Lombard-Italian. He had just been reading Milton's " Paradise Lost " in an Italian version, and soon made up his mind to learn the English language so as to read the great masterpiece of literature in the original. His first literary successes were achieved as a lecturer, and his name appeared for the first time in a non-ecclesiastical book of reference in Count Angelo de Gubernatis's " Dictionnaire International des Écrivains du Monde Latin " (1905) as :

"Ratti, Achille, prêtre et historien italien, membre effectif de l'Institut Lombard de sciences et lettres et Conseiller de la Société Historique Lombarde de Milan."

The present Pope's most interesting published volumes, apart from purely ecclesiastical, are mainly historical, and the most important are: "Al monta Rosa, punta Dufour da Macugnaga e prima traversata dell colle Zumstein" (1890); "Contribuzione alla storia eucaristica di Milano" (1895); "Del monaco cisterciense don Ermete Bonomi, milanese, e le sue opere" (1895); "La Miscellanea Chiaravallese" (1895); "Il più antico rittrato di S. Ambrogio" (1897); "Ancora del celebre cod. MS. delle opere di Virgilio già di F. Petrarca ed ora della Biblioteca Ambrosiana, Milano" (1904); his edition (with A. M. Geriani as co-editor) of "Homeri Iliadis pictae fragmenta Ambrosiana" (1905, obl. 4°); his edition of the "Vita di Bonacosa de Beccaloe, 1352-1381" (1909); his edition of his friend A. M. Geriani's

" Miscellanea " (1910), and his edition of Cardinal Baronius's " Opuscolo inedito," which contains a large number of interesting notes. This great Cardinal, who died at Rome in 1607, was librarian at the Vatican, like his posthumous editor the present Pope.

His Holiness Pope Pius XI., unlike his immediate predecessor, Benedict XV., is not of noble birth, and cannot claim remote princely ancestors, but his family have been connected with literature for more than two centuries. Giulio Cesare Ratti, a distinguished historian of the Catholic Church, was responsible for " Rittratto della santa vita del glorioso S. Francesco Borgia," etc. (Milano, 1671).

Carlo Giuseppe Ratti published several works on painting, sculpture, and architecture between 1766 and 1781. The best-known works of Nicola Ratti are : " Della Famiglia Sforza " (two parts, 1794-1795) ; " Storia di Genzano con note e documenti " (Roma, 1797), and " Su la Vita di Giusto, Conti

Romani, poeta volgare del secolo XV."
(1824).

Giovanni Maria Ratti had one of his
works translated into English as " The
Good Mother of a Family occupied with
her Children in the Practice of Christian
Piety " (London, 1849). The journalist
Vincenzio Ratti was editor of the *Cotti-
diano d'Arti* (1869), and the *Corriere
Astigiano* (1871-1876). He also published in volume form " I melodrammi
di Pietro Metastasio " (1864), and " Carlo
Goldoni, Discorsi " (1874). Luigi Ratti
was a distinguished lawyer in Lombardy,
and also achieved much success as a
dramatist and opera librettist. His publications include a libretto based on Shakes-
peare's " Much Ado About Nothing,"
and the beautiful poetical play " Raffa-
ello e la Fornarina " (1879). Cosmo
Ratti was responsible for " Delle giuris-
dizioni ne' diversi stati Italiani della fine
del secolo XVIII." (1887). The twentieth-
century members include F. V. Ratti,
who made a contribution to the late
Great War literature with " L'Adria-

tico degli altri . . . con 37 illustrazioni
fotografiche . . . e una geografica dell'
Albania " (Firenze, 1915).

It will be remembered that Sir Thomas
Hall Caine, in " The Eternal City " (1901),
styled his " Pope " in the novel and play
" Pius X.," and on the election of the
real Pope Pius X., altered it to " Pius
XI." This is the title of the present
Pope. It is a pity the distinguished
novelist did not select the now rarely
used titles of John, Sixtus, or Clement.

CHAPTER THREE

ASCENT OF MONTE ROSA (DUFOUR PEAK)
FROM MACUGNAGA, AND FIRST TRA-
VERSE OF THE ZUMSTEINJOCH*

THE *Monthly Review* of the Italian
Alpine Club for August, 1889, contained a short notice of this expedition,
announcing it as " the first Italian traverse
of Monte Rosa from Macugnaga to
Zermatt."

The *Gazette Piémontaise* had mentioned
it under the same title in its issue of
August 23rd.

I am grateful—on behalf of those who
were with me on the climb, as well as
on my own—for this announcement, the

* The following account of this notable exped-
ition was contributed by His Holiness (then
Dr. Ratti) to the *Bollettino* of the Italian Alpine
Club for 1889, vol. xxiii., No. 56, pp. 1-29.

accuracy of which we do not see any reason to doubt.

As, moreover, the *Review* concluded the notice with the remark that a detailed account of our climb was expected, I shall now do my best to meet its wishes. I am the more anxious to do so as the aforesaid notice, derived from a summary, hastily written on my return from the climb to satisfy the express desire of the editor for an early report, was much too incomplete and lacking in detail, especially with regard to the route on the descent. It merely stated that from the Dufour peak we started down towards Zermatt, and nothing more; whereas the route we followed, which was long, possibly incorrect, but certainly most interesting, possessed another advantage, far greater than any which was found, and promptly pointed out, in our *ascent* of the highest peak—namely, that of being the first by *Italian* climbers : I mean the advantage of being new with regard to mountaineering generally.

I venture to call attention to it with all

the more confidence, now that I have had the opportunity of studying profitably the accounts and the known facts concerning the most notable expeditions that have been carried out in the main Monte Rosa group.

These particulars cannot fail to be of interest and of use to all who practise mountain ascents.

In the early days of June, 1889, in agreement with my colleague, dearest of friends, and now my old and tried climbing companion, Professor Sacerdote Luigi Grasselli, who, like myself, was a member of the Milan section, I wrote to Giuseppe Gadin, the Courmayeur guide, asking him to be at Macugnaga by July 28th, and promising to join him there on the morning of the 29th.

We intended to cross the Weissthor, and, after ascending the Cima di Jazzi, to descend to Zermatt, and then . . . But we had also decided, if necessary, to abandon the whole of this plan and what might have followed, in favour of an ascent of the Dufour peak (the highest point of Monte Rosa) from Macugnaga.

We kept our idea in the background, however, both in order to avoid exposing it to the danger of an argument, which at that early date might have developed into a lengthy one, and to ensure its meeting with a good reception, if brought forward on the spot and in favourable circumstances.

Gadin in his reply, however, stole a march on us, as the saying is, and rendered any reserve on our part quite unnecessary.

"It is understood," he wrote to me, "that I shall be at Macugnaga on the 28th of July (next month).

"But please take notice that if the weather is fine we are going up Monte Rosa."

I need not say what our final reply was ; and in the meantime we agreed that Gadin should bring with him his fellow-villager Alessio Proment, a strong, intelligent young man whose name was inscribed among the Courmayeur guides, but who was prepared to come with us as a porter.

We certainly knew that neither of the

two men, like ourselves, had ever ascended the Dufour peak by any route, and we also knew that it was not an expedition to be lightly undertaken.

Three years before, the stones set up in the cemetery at Macugnaga in memory of Marinelli and Imseng, together with the detailed account of the terrible accident in which they had met their deaths, had made a very painful impression on me; and I was familiar with the narratives and the short notices which had appeared in the various Alpine reviews with reference to the previous ascents of the Dufour peak from Macugnaga.

It had, however, appeared to me that the dangers met with on those ascents, dangers which had not always been braved with impunity, were reasonably attributable to unfavourable conditions of the mountain and the weather.

As for us, in the first place we knew our men. It was just a year since we had attempted with these very guides the ascent of Mont Blanc from Courmayeur. Our party had consisted of Professor

Grasselli and myself, together with my brother Edward, a member, like ourselves, of the Milan section.

We were besieged by bad weather in the Sella hut, and a lack of both food and fuel obliged us to come down in the teeth of wind and snow; and it was just in that descent that our men inspired us with boundless confidence in them. Our trust will not seem excessive to anyone who knows the locality, and can imagine it deeply covered with snow a long way below the platform on which stands the old hut, now no longer in use.

I think a short historical review of previous ascents of Monte Rosa by the east face will be of use in making the position clear.

As early as 1867, Messrs. Mathews and Morshead were examining the east face of Monte Rosa from the Pizzo Bianco, which stands facing it to the south of Macugnaga, and formed the idea of attacking the giant on that side. They did not, however, carry out their plan, because they considered it too dangerous at that time, on account of the avalanches which fell without ceasing from below the highest point.

The same idea was taken up by Mr. Taylor and Messrs. Pendlebury, who were the first to put it into execution, on the 22nd of July, 1872.

In No. 41 (vol. vi.) of the *Alpine Journal* is printed the paper read by Mr. Taylor himself before the Alpine Club in London on the 2nd of April, 1873, and Signor Cerruti of the Varallo section gave a translation of it in the *Journal of the C. A. I.* for 1875 (p. 87).

One need only read that paper in order to realise how the width of the crevasses on the upper glacier and the continual threat of avalanches hindered the climbers' advance, and filled them at times with absolute terror.

The same ascent was accomplished successfully, though not without danger from falling stones and threatened avalanches, by Herr Lendenfeld of Graz on the 9th of August, 1880, and an account was written by him in the

Oesterreichische Alpen Zeitung for 1881, No. 67.

Our much regretted fellow-member Damiano Marinelli (of the Florence section) did not think it right that it should be left to foreigners to attempt and accomplish, on the Italian side, the ascent of Monte Rosa, which has been rightly described as being essentially Italian, just as the Matterhorn is essentially Swiss.

In the summer of 1881 he was at Macugnaga ; but conditions could not have been more unfavourable—nay, more hostile—to him : the scirocco (*Föhn*) prevailed and the avalanches were almost incessant. Mr. Mathews was right in saying that neglect of the most elementary precautions was followed by its natural result. On the 8th of August poor Marinelli was the victim of an avalanche in the great couloir, or gully, which still bears his name, and which, till another route is discovered, must still be crossed to reach the Dufour peak. Another foreigner, Professor Schulz of Leipzig, in no wise daunted by the sad occurrence, next attempted the climb and, helped by exceptionally favourable conditions, accomplished it successfully, and gave a short account of it in the *S. A. C. Journal* (vol. xix., p. 527) and in the *Oesterreichische Alpen Zeitung* (1884, p. 69).

His unexpected success inspired the brothers Zsigmondy with, perhaps, excessive confidence, and they made the venture with Herr Purtscheller, and without guides, on the 12th, 13th, and 14th of August, 1884.

They were successful indeed, but in the face of the gravest dangers, due to the bad weather and the frequent falls of ice and stones.

I think so much is evident from the account which was sent by one of the Zsigmondys to the *Oesterreichische Alpen Zeitung* and forthwith translated and summarised in the *Review* of the C. A. I. (1885, p. 82) by our fellow-member Count F. Lurani, at that time secretary of the Milan section.

A fresh attempt was made on the 16th and 17th of July, 1885, by Herr Strauss

with Ranggetiner as guide. A stone hit
the guide near the rocks of the summit,
and Herr Strauss found himself obliged
to descend the Marinelli couloir amid the
most serious dangers; happily, however, he succeeded in saving himself and
the wounded guide. How he would
have blessed the Marinelli hut now built
there may be seen from his account in
the *Oesterreichische Touristen Zeitung* (1885,
No. 19).

Meanwhile, on the Jägerrücken, not
far from the spot where Marinelli lost
his life, but in a perfectly safe place, at
about 3,100 metres, the Milan section
was building the hut which there also
keeps green the memory of that ill-fated
climber who had done so much in the
past for mountaineering.

The Marinelli hut was opened on the
5th of August, 1886, and the *Rivista* for
that year gave a full account of the
opening ceremony (p. 327).

The first to use it for the ascent of the
Dufour Spitze were, as far as I know,
Signor Prohaska and Signor Kugy of

Trieste, who accomplished two separate expeditions, the former on the 6th, and the latter on the 12th and 13th of August in that year (1886). The *Mittheilungen des D. Œ. A. V.* (1886, No. 17, p. 205) contained a brief account of these climbs. Signor Prohaska had a cold night with no avalanches, while Signor Kugy heard them falling all night.

Both climbers found the glacier in excellent condition, but met with great difficulties on the topmost ridge, the former owing to freshly fallen snow, the latter to verglas.

Again, we must not leave out the first traverse from Macugnaga to Zermatt, accomplished by Dr. Blodig, with the above-mentioned Ranggetiner, on the 6th of August, 1880, by the col, which lies at a height of 4,490 metres to the north of the Dufour, between that peak and the Nordend. He named it the Ranggetinerjoch in honour of his excellent guide : it is the same as the one usually called the Silbersattel. The traverse was successful, but much hampered by bad weather. I should refer also to the first and perhaps, so far, the only ascent of the Nordend combined with the traverse of the Jägerjoch, which was accomplished by Signor Brioschi of the Milan section; but I have been unable to find any detailed account of it, and I have not seen the terms of the short report on the climb which was left, if I mistake not, by Signor Brioschi himself at the Monte Rosa Hotel at Macugnaga.

Another expedition which also belongs to the list of ascents of Monte Rosa on the east side is the traverse of the Jägerhorn, which was first done by the abovementioned Messrs. Mathews and Morshead on the 17th of July, 1867.

The same traverse was accomplished on August 23rd, 1887, by Herr Curtius of the Berne section of the S. A. C., but, as he points out, by a route that was at least partly new, and after an interval of twenty years between Mathews' ascent and his, during which time, as far as he knew, the idea of traversing the Monte Rosa range had not been carried out again.

As a matter of fact, however, as early as August, 1884, two members of the Milan section, Avvocato Magnaghi and the aforesaid Signor Brioschi had done the same climb, and by the same route, with Clement Imseng of Macugnaga as guide. No public account of this was ever given, as far as I know, so that Herr Curtius cannot be charged with any inaccuracy ; nevertheless, the fact is none the less certain. Equally certain is it that, on August 6th, 1886, Avvocato Paolo Palestrina and Signor Luigi Simondetti, both of the Turin section, together with Antonio Castagneri of Balme d' Ala as guide, after being the first to spend the night in the Marinelli hut, traversed the Jägergletscher from south to north, reached the rock ridge which descends from the Jägerhorn, and by its means arrived within about 50 metres of the summit, whence they made their way down to the col (Jägerjoch), and from there to Zermatt ; they had been dissuaded from attempting the ascent of the Dufour peak by the great quantity of fresh snow. Let this suffice : if any name or any expedition has been left out, I hope the omission will not be attributed to intentional negligence, but on the one hand to my lack of knowledge, and on the other to a want of time to make the list more complete.

As far as we were concerned, there was no need of so many previous experiments to assure us that what we required above all was to find the glacier unbroken and the weather fine and cold.

The former condition would save us from the trouble caused by crevasses, the latter from the danger of avalanches ; and we should be very lucky not to find a quantity of fresh snow or verglas on the rocks of the summit.

These, I hasten to add, are the conditions which will always be quite indispensable to anyone wishing in the future to attempt and carry out this expedition, not, indeed, without difficulty, which is impossible, but without danger. Not one of these conditions was lacking to us or failed us at any time.

But before we proceed further, perhaps those of my readers—if I have any—who may not know the locality would like me to give some idea of it.

In order to meet their wishes briefly and accurately, I will make use of the aforesaid narrative of Herr Zsigmondy; I quote as much of it as is necessary from Lurani's excellent translation, a very few slight variations excepted:

" The gigantic eastern face of the Monte Rosa massif is crowned by four summits: the Nordend (4,612 metres), Dufour peak (4,638 metres), Zumstein-spitze (4,573 metres), and Signalkuppe (4,561 metres)."

I venture to add that the expression " massif " is well chosen; because there are, belonging likewise to Monte Rosa, though not to its central portion, quite six other peaks, all of them, with one exception, over 4,000 metres high—namely, to the north of the first four, the Jägerhorn (3,972 metres); to the south, the Parrotspitze (4,434 metres), the Ludwigshöhe (4,346 metres), the Schwarzhorn (4,334 metres), the Vincent Pyramide

(4,215 metres), and the Punta Giordani (4,055 metres).

" From the foot of the wall, right in the middle of the steep ice slope, two ridges run up towards the summits.

" The northern one is called the Jäger-rücken, the southern is the Imsengrücken.

" The former, which is under the Nor-dend, is narrower, starts lower down, and attains to a lesser height; the latter, under the Dufour peak, is broader and steeper, but is quite smooth and resembles a wall from which the glacier has retreated, rather than a ridge of rock.

" It is on the Jägerrücken, in absolute security from avalanches, that aspirants to Monte Rosa usually pass the night (and it was precisely on these rocks that, as is recorded by the translator, the Marinelli hut was built).

" Between the aforesaid two ' Rücken ' lies a fairly deep couloir, down which must necessarily come all the stones which break away from the loose rocks of the Nordend and the fragments of the ice and snow cornices above.

" The traverse of this couloir is, there-fore, particularly feared on account of the avalanches which follow one another at short intervals throughout the day."

If this last statement may be said to be true as a rule, it is certain that the rule is subject to some happy exceptions, as is that other which is elsewhere quoted as a rule, and on very sound data—namely, the statement that the avalanches on the east face of Monte Rosa are usually most frequent at one in the morning.

That there are such exceptions is shown by some of the accounts referred to above. The writer had previously had ocular demonstration of them on the spot in the course of his expeditions to the Pedriolo Alp, and to the Cima di Jazzi, with his brave young friend Daniele Corsi, three years before the present ascent; and a further proof was to be supplied by the expedition itself. Moreover, we had every reason beforehand to expect such exception, thanks to the special conditions with which we were favoured.

I include among these circumstances a heavy squall, which, two days before our arrival at Macugnaga, had travelled from north to south above the village and had gone off on the Pizzo Bianco side.

The temperature had in consequence, undergone a decided drop, and any stone or sérac which might have been in a condition of doubtful balance must certainly have come down: it remained to be seen whether any fresh snow had fallen, and if so, how much. Meanwhile the storm had been followed by weather that was not only fine, but splendid, and when Monte Rosa displayed itself to us on the road from Venzone to Prequartero, it was a spectacle of incomparable beauty. Around us was the fresh green of the meadows and the woods; above us the canopy of heaven, tinged with the most beautiful blue that was ever seen, of a truly crystalline purity and transparency; and in front towered the Alpine giant, inviting or defying—I hardly know which—with the immense extent of its snow and ice, with the mighty crown of its ten peaks rising to heights of 4,000 to 4,600 metres and more, sparkling and flaming in the rosy rays of the rising sun.

We arrived at Pestarena, where a large gang of workers in the gold mines, who had already finished their first meal, were about to return down the shafts.

It is noteworthy how the English, with their practical ability and characteristic courage, contrive to employ profitably considerable capital in that outlying part of Italy. I say considerable capital, not only on account of the importance of the works and the number of men employed, but also (to the praise of the English be it said) because of the liberality with which they ensure the safety of our workmen, who elsewhere are often sacrificed to a murderous economy.

Thanks to a courteous letter of introduction from the British Consulate at Milan, and the kindness of the captains of the mine (for so they are called by the miners, who are under a kind of military régime), we were enabled to witness the principal operations of the mine, and to see the king of metals extracted from the *pesta arena*, or crushed sand, as the name of the place (Pestarena) would seem to indicate.

It might have been about 8.30 in the morning, and Pestarena was not far behind us, when our men came into view. They were not expecting to see us arrive so early, but our first greetings were none the less cordial for that. " Well, gentlemen, there is Monte Rosa, and we are going up it," said Gadin, almost immediately, going straight to the heart of the matter.

So, as far as he was concerned, the expedition was settled, and the good fellow had already done something to ensure its success.

He had arrived at Macugnaga a full day before us, and had not wasted his time, but had employed it most usefully in collecting information and in reconnoitring the route on the spot, having been with Proment nearly up to the Pedriolo Alp. With that intuition, I might almost say that prophetic instinct, which distinguishes really great guides, he had made out the whole route to be followed from the Marinelli hut to the Dufour peak.

As far as the eye and the glass could discern, not a single large crevasse, not one dangerous hanging cornice could be seen, not a sign of troublesome fresh snow or a trace of verglas on the rocks of the summit : the principal crevasse (Bergschrund) was hardly visible.

When we arrived at the Monte Moro Hotel, we found that our project had already obtained a most encouraging vote of confidence. The landlord of the hotel, Signor Giovanni Oberto, had ascended the Dufour peak with the first English party (Mr. Taylor's), and had already made the acquaintance of our men. "In weather like this and with men like those," he said to me, "you can certainly go."

I have expatiated somewhat on these preliminaries in order to show that the idea of attempting a gambler's throw, as it is called, never entered our heads. Indeed, it really seems to me that if on the whole we were lucky, we were not at all rash, or even, strictly speaking, venturesome.

I say this, not because I think it necessary for real mountaineers who may read what I have written, but rather, if I may use the expression, for the uninitiated.

Is it, however, possible to convince the latter, as the former are firmly convinced, that mountaineering is not a breakneck pursuit, but that it is, on the contrary, merely a question of prudence and of a little courage, of love of Nature and her most secret beauties—beauties which are sometimes awful, but are at those times all the more sublime and life-giving to the spirit of him who contemplates them?

"Why do men go up on to the heights?" One of the greatest writers whom the Alps have inspired asks this question of himself, and that which follows reveals the true and enthusiastic mountaineer :

"Is it perchance a mysterious inexplicable fascination, which leads him to defy mortal perils at every step, to risk his brave but fragile life on vast and lonely expanses of ice ; often to find shelter with difficulty in a miserable hut against the raging storm and the deadly frost, in order finally, hanging between life and death, gasping for breath and trembling in every limb, to attain the narrow summit of some snowy peak, majestic as a monarch on his throne?

" Or is it perhaps merely the desire to boast of his prowess—a poor reward for almost superhuman labour—that beckons him to the region of the clouds ?   We find it difficult to believe as much.

" It is rather a longing to know his beloved native land even to its utmost boundaries and its highest summits, with its indescribable natural beauties.

" It is the feeling in him of his spiritual energy which inspires him and drives him to overcome the terrors of lifeless matter ; it is the desire to measure man's individual faculties, the infinite power of intelligent free-will, with the brute forces of the elements ; it is the sacred instinct which bids us explore in the service of science the inmost structure and life of the earth, the mysterious organism of all created things ; it is, perhaps, the ambition of the lord of the earth to seal with a vigorous act of his own volition his relationship with the Infinite, on the highest point ,which he has at last attained, and whence his glance can sweep over the world which lies at his feet."

We stopped at Macugnaga long enough to rest ourselves and to pay a short visit to its interesting, lonely little church ; and another, still shorter, to the parish priest, whose cordial hospitality we are undoubtedly not the only ones to remember.

May this simple and hasty mention serve as our thanks to him, not only for his kindness to us at Macugnaga, but also for the anxiety—I had almost called it brotherly—with which armed with his telescope, he kept us in view for a great part of our long ascent.

Shortly before 1 o'clock we started for the Marinelli hut, and, greeted on our way by a herd of chamois, arrived there at about 7 in the evening, without encountering any difficulty, except a terrible sleepiness, which came upon the writer just at the wrong time, and against which, though Gadin's excellent arguments were of no use, a very few drops of ammonia proved a sovereign remedy.

The phenomenon caused me no surprise. It is no rare one in the mountains ; it seemed to me natural enough after my sudden change from low-lying Milan to the height of nearly 3,000 metres ; and I had, from my previous ex-

perience, every confidence in the final
effects of the mountain on my personal
well-being. I may add that my faith
was eventually proved to be completely
justified.

At the hut we were confronted with an
inconvenience which was, indeed, not
serious, but very tiresome. We found it
imperfectly closed and encumbered with
snow ; it contained, perhaps, 2 or 3 cubic
metres, congealed, and looking as if it
had been thrown in one solid block.

It may be easily imagined with what
expressions we gazed upon it, anxious as
we were to refresh and warm ourselves at
a fire without delay. However, thanks
to a wise division of labour, the intruding
snow was soon cast out, and we were able
to feel ourselves the masters.

Boiled snow and Liebig's extract of
meat formed the most useful, though not
the only, ingredients of our supper, while
we went out in turn to forecast the
weather and to admire the beauty of the
scene which the evening was revealing to
us in our lofty abode.

Solemn silence reigned around, the stars shone brightly in the infinite azure, almost velvety sky, the huge masses of the mountains and their sublime summits towered in majesty about us, and their gigantic shadows stretched forth and intermingled on the white expanses of snow and ice.

It was not till 11 o'clock that we lay down on the hard boards which constituted our only beds, and, needless to say, went off to sleep.

That sleep was sweet, but all too short, because at 1 o'clock Gadin awakened us as agreed, and in a few seconds the whole of the little party was afoot. Not one avalanche had disturbed our brief rest, and the cold and the fine weather were with us still; so the word was: Forward!

In order to ensure against any possibility, let alone any positive danger, of avalanches, we had decided to cross the Marinelli couloir by night, so as to be certain of clearing it, even if the passage should prove difficult, before the sun could shine on the snow and ice above. Such a proceeding naturally entails some discomfort and some increase of precautions on the route, but we still think it most advisable.

One of the most necessary of these precautions is the possession of good lanterns, and we had two.

After making the needful changes in our attire, and comforting the inner man with Liebig broth and hot wine, we carefully extinguished the fire, firmly closed the hut, and put on the rope.

Gadin tied himself on first with the greatest care, then I, and after me Proment, with Professor Grasselli last, and we kept this order throughout.

Proment carried one of the lanterns, Gadin the other, as long as we were on the rocks. But we were soon to leave these behind us, for, a short distance above the hut, we found ourselves at the edge of the famous couloir.

We had intended to cross the latter diagonally, in an upward direction, and we did not expect much trouble in reaching the rocks of the Imsengrücken, which loomed darkly in front of us.

Gadin passed the lantern to me, and we all jumped after him on to the snow. But our luck was out! Underneath a thin crust, it was so soft, that we sank in up to our knees. After careful scrutiny, Gadin came to the conclusion that it was a question of a local accumulation of snow, due to a recent avalanche; and the event proved him to be right.

We were forced to descend somewhat, to try and find a better route; but meanwhile the length of our diagonal traverse of the couloir was necessarily much increased. As soon as Signor Oberto became aware of this, he said at once, and rightly, that our climb would be greatly prolonged; and it was destined to be lengthened even more! For, after descending for a while, we found the snow not only firm, but excessively hard.

Here was another drawback, especially for Gadin, who had not expected to begin cutting steps so early.

Poor Gadin! When I think that he

persevered at this hard work for nearly the whole of that long day, without ever consenting to give up his place to anyone else, I am still amazed at his muscles of steel and his endurance.

And we were soon to make another unpleasant discovery. The great couloir proved to consist of an endless series of smaller gullies, which enormously increased the length and the difficulty of our traverse. I have not found any mention of this peculiarity in any of the accounts of previous ascents, and it is perhaps the absence of this condition and of the others aforesaid which explains why others had crossed the couloir in so much less time than we did.

We were obliged continually to go up and down, and down and up, making very little progress with respect to the width of the main couloir, while the lanterns were constantly disappearing from view behind the ridges which separated the various gullies, and Gadin's voice was often heard calmly saying to us : "Prenez garde, Messieurs, c'est un mauvais pas."

Gadin, who speaks excellent Italian and can even hold his own in English, seems, in serious situations, to prefer a French of his own, like many others in the Val d' Aosta, and even more at Courmayeur.

And in the meantime our eyes travelled instinctively up and down the steep couloir, always, however, returning eagerly to the rocks of the Imsengrücken.

After struggling on for at least an hour and a half, we seemed to be still in the very middle of the couloir, and the rocks as far off and unattainable as ever, while we could not help thinking—though we ourselves felt perfectly safe—of poor Marinelli and the accident in which he had lost his life hard by.

By God's goodwill, we at last laid hands upon the rocks, and we felt like the shipwrecked mariner of whom Dante's lines give a description so true, but so well known, that it is happily unnecessary to quote them.

We halted for a short quarter of an hour, and had a drink of wine or coffee, I cannot remember which; and then we

began to climb as straight as possible up
the rocks, which end in a narrow ridge
between the couloir and the upper glacier.
And all would have been well if this rock
ridge had been continuous ; for a ridge
of good rock like this, however steep it
may be, always offers firm and relatively
easy holds.   The trouble was that, about
5 or 6 metres from the edge of the glacier,
the ridge dropped suddenly down into a
gap, whose sides were excessively steep
and smooth.

The difficulty would perhaps have
proved insurmountable had it not been
for a narrow snow arête, which rose
light and slender from the base of the
precipice, and bridged the gap between
rock and glacier.

The passage was clearly none of the
best, but there was no other, and, moreover, the snow, though very thin, was
firm and almost as solid as ice ; and,
after all, its whole length was no more
than that of the rope between two of us,
and, as all experts know, there is no
passage which cannot, in such conditions,

be attempted with prudence and safety.

" Tenez-moi la corde, Monsieur," said Gadin to me with decision, after a short consultation. And while the others and I, standing firmly on the rock, followed him with our eyes, our hands on the rope, and all of us ready to assist him, he accomplished the traverse with a truly admirable security and sangfroid.

Keeping the top of the ridge level with his thigh, he placed his feet down where the two slopes began to deviate somewhat from the vertical, thus adding a little to the thickness of the wall.

In this way, avoiding the frozen snow on one side, and resting his axe lightly on the other, he passed over successfully, and took up his position on the glacier.

A traverse which might well be sufficiently difficult for the first man was not at all so for the others, and in fact we all went over without any incident but a halt of a minute or two right in the middle of the writer's acrobatic performance, which halt was imposed on him by Gadin, who no doubt felt the need of taking up a still firmer position on the glacier.

The situation must have been most serious in our brave guide's opinion, because, when I found the unpleasant halt lasting too long, and asked him whether I might proceed, he replied, without even turning round : " Monsieur, je vous en prie, ne parlez pas ; cela me dérange l'esprit."

When we were all across, we started over the glacier, bearing for some time to the left, and making our way up between the Zumstein and Dufour peaks ; next, we turned to the right, towards the rocks of the final peak. This again added to the length of our route, which, however, became safer with every step we took away from the Nordend, provided we did not approach the Zumstein too closely.

As regards crevasses, we could not have hoped to find the glacier in better condition, so smooth and unbroken was it ; but this advantage was unfortunately counterbalanced by the fact that the

glacier was covered with a coating of
snow, which was not deep or firm enough
to bear our weight, and made it necessary
to cut steps in the hard ice, adding very
greatly to our labour.

Partly on this account, and partly
because of the general steepness of the
icy slopes, we advanced slowly; still, we
gained height continually, at times
climbing straight up, at others taking
long zigzags.

After several hours of silent, careful
climbing we halted at a short distance
from the Bergschrund, in the shadow of
a huge, massive wall of pure ice, whose
brow projected and extended above our
heads a regular crystal canopy; a number
of icicles hung down like a fringe of
enormous diamonds from its outer edge.

For the first time since our departure
from the hut, we looked at our watches:
it was about 1 p.m.

So we had already been climbing for
twelve hours—no less—with no real halt,
except the one on the Imsengrücken. We
were entitled to a little rest, and we took

it where we were, sitting on the snow, gazing at the sublime beauty of Nature, and restoring our strength with Suchard chocolate, which we found then and afterwards a real godsend; not that we lacked other food, but our stomachs did not seem inclined to absorb anything else.

I do not remember looking at the aneroid that I had with me, but we thought we could not be very far from our goal; indeed, the rocks of the Dufour looked very near.

In point of fact, this was a real optical illusion, which was perhaps at that time accentuated by the clearness of the atmosphere, but which frequently occurs in the high mountains. Everything is there on a large scale, the surrounding peaks and the distances between them, the general outlines of the landscape, and the details. But, for this very reason, the great size of the component parts is not exactly concealed, but is in some measure transformed and merged in the harmonious whole.

For that matter, the same occurs in the great works of human art : the mountaineer who has seen San Pietro in Vaticano and Bernini's colonnade, both of them so huge, yet so graceful and harmonious, so diverse in their separate parts, yet so easy in their grand simplicity, to assemble under the eye in one comprehensive view —that mountaineer knows that here, too, it is ever in the imitation of Nature that our art shows closest kinship with that of God, the first Creator of all beautiful things.

But none of us had just then a thought for such matters as these. We felt certain that in another couple of hours we should reach the summit, and that very evening (no matter how late) rest on our laurels, or, in other words, sleep in the comfortable beds of the Riffel and among all its comforts, which we should doubly appreciate.

But the snow, which had already delayed us so much in the Marinelli couloir and on the glacier in a manner dissimilar but equally effective in each, was about to do us the same ill-turn and on a greater scale.

Having taken breath, we now started once more, and, adopting a route which was not the shortest to the rocks of the summit but possessed the advantage of not being overhung with masses of ice, at an hour when these are most exposed to the heat of the sun and most likely to break off in avalanches, we were obliged to attack an ice-wall which rose perpendicularly on our left. Though only a few metres in height, it took us at least half an hour to climb, and we had to use every trick of hand and foot. It was, perhaps, at this point that the watchers with their telescopes at Macugnaga thought we were stationary for too long, and began to fear for the safety of the party.

Once we had passed this place, only a snow slope of moderate steepness lay between us and the rocks.

We began to attack it; but lo! the rocks appeared to recede as we advanced towards them, and the summit seemed to rise higher and higher, and to grow more and more difficult of access.

The illusion vanished, and gave place to reality, the reality being that we had yet a long way to go before reaching the summit.

The snow, moreover, became softer and softer and more and more yielding, so that we were soon no longer walking, but painfully and constantly stumbling.

Anyone who has happened to walk in deep snow will understand how greatly our advance was again hindered and checked.

Gadin admitted to me later that at this point he had almost given up hope of reaching the summit on the same day, and that he had thought of looking out for a place of refuge for the night on the lowest rocks. He did not, however, mention it at the time, and, all things considered, it was just as well.

At last we touched solid ground; we reached the rocks!

The nearer we approached to our goal, the keener became our eagerness to reach it, and the sun, which was steadily sinking towards the horizon, warned us that we had not a moment to lose. And how about our promised rest? and where were we to pass the night?

No one alluded to the difficulty, which all could see.

The Zsigmondy brothers had spent more than one night on that face, and in very different weather, and it is well known that whole nights have been passed with impunity on the very summit of the Matterhorn and even of Mont Blanc.

We attacked the rocks by the ridge which runs down right above the Imsengrücken.

It is easier to imagine than to describe the means by which we climbed the bare slabs and the masses of reddish gneiss which form the summit.

I shall only mention one incident which befell my friend, and which was bound to entail consequences that were, indeed, not serious, but of long duration and only lately ended. At a given place I heard him cry out . . . I turned round and saw his axe flying like an arrow from the bow down the rocks on to the nearest snowfields.

What was to be done? We were not in a position even to make an attempt at its recovery. We would have thought of doing so; but meanwhile Professor Grasselli was obliged that evening and next morning to put his hands on the cold rocks and in the snow more than was convenient. His gloves were soon torn to pieces, and became quite useless to him; the final result was, severe frost-bite in the fleshy parts of his fingers of which he was not completely cured till some months later, by the heat of Milan.

None but a mountaineer of Professor Grasselli's skill and courage could have borne and overcome the difficulties caused by this incident, as he did throughout this expedition.

The giant, being now near defeat, began to assail us with his spite and vengeance.

Soon after, the wind arose, and with such violence, that Professor Grasselli's hat (Monte Rosa evidently had a most unpleasant partiality for him), though firmly secured, flew off on to the glacier, followed at short intervals by mine and Proment's ; Gadin's was reserved for the wrath of the Matterhorn. Our woollen caps replaced our hats.

But now our efforts were crowned with success.

It must have been about 7.30 p.m. when we were all assembled on the Ostspitze of the top of Monte Rosa.

I shall not expend a single word in description of that unforgettable instant, and of what we saw and felt. The memory of such moments speaks with unequalled eloquence to the elect ; whereas no words could suffice or even be credible to others.

We had every reason to believe that our undertaking was, in the main, accomplished. We postponed to the following morning our ascent of the other peak, more particularly called the Allerhöchste, or Dufourspitze, which, together with the Ostspitze, forms the summit of Monte Rosa. It was too late in the day to venture on a passage such as lay before us.

When I say that we could consider the ascent as *in the main* accomplished, my expression may confuse a good many of my readers (if indeed I have more than a very few) ; and in order to clear up any doubts, I shall allow myself to digress a little.

The highest summit of Monte Rosa is undoubtedly, as is usually stated, and as I have already mentioned, a double tooth of rock. The most easterly is called the Ostspitze, the other the Allerhöchstespitze.

It is not, however, equally certain (or it was not formerly so considered by all) that the indication given by the names is correct, and that the Ostspitze is lower than the other point.

Mr. Freshfield, formerly editor of the *Alpine Journal* in London, and a distinguished mountaineer, refers to this point in a note appended to the abovementioned paper by Mr. Taylor.

It will be useful to quote his words :

" The Ost Spitze of Monte Rosa mentioned by Mr. Taylor is undoubtedly the
summit above the Silber-Sattel (the hollow
between Monte Rosa proper and the Nord
end), ascended in 1848 by Professor
Ulrich's guides, and subsequently by other
parties, who, without any sufficient reason,
considered it impracticable to pass from it
to the Dufour, or as it is more generally
called, the Allerhöchste Spitze.   After the
reading of Mr. Taylor's paper, a discussion
took place as to the relative height of the
two peaks, and Mr. Moore suggested that
the Allerhöchste Spitze may prove to be in
reality the lower of the two.   The difference in height between them is, as we can
testify by experience, exceedingly small,
and not easily determined by the eye.

" For, having climbed Monte Rosa by
the ordinary route, but with guides
strange to the mountain, at a time when
the stone man on the Dufour Spitze was
masked by a heavy fall of fresh snow, we
walked over that summit, and began without a question the passage of the ridge
leading on to the eastern peak.*

* The note here quoted refers to an ascent of
Monte Rosa I made in 1869 with Sir F. Pollock.
As far as I remember, the stone man marking the

" Some progress had been made, when one of the party, looking back, detected the stone man, to which we then returned.

" Standing on the Dufour Spitze, it seemed to us impossible to assert with confidence its superior height. But, on the other hand, all those who have reached the eastern summit have, despite the natural bias they must have felt towards a contrary opinion, acquiesced in its inferiority.

" The question, now attention has been called to it, admits of easy decision, but we shall be urprised if the established verdict is reversed." (*Alpine Journal*, vol. vi., No. 41).

Seeing that we were on the Ostspitze in the evening of the 30th, and again in the morning of the 31st, and that we crossed over from it to the Dufour and back again in the course of a few hours, our opinion may be of some little value.

summit at that date was on a platform a little below the highest crag. The question raised here has been set at rest by the Swiss official measurements, as follows: The Dufourspitze, 4,638 metres; Ostspitze, 4,633 metres; Grenz Gipfel the knob where the spur and watershed meet), 4,631 metres (see *Alpine Journal*, vol. xxix., p. 141).

D. W. F.

For this reason we express it, without putting forth any claim whatsoever, either to decide the question or to establish or reverse verdicts of any kind.

It seemed then to all of us that here, too, the truth lay half-way between the two extremes of opinion, as expressed by different observers.

I say " seemed," because, in the case of such a relatively minute difference of level, it would be unreasonable to bring forward the evidence of a small aneroid, which could not measure such difference, and could not be considered a very accurate instrument.

All the same, it really did appear to us, first, that the Ostspitze is not the highest ; secondly, that neither is the stone man on the Dufour at the highest point ; thirdly, that between the Ostspitze and the stone man, and quite close to the latter, there is another point, which is very slightly higher than the stone man, and considerably higher than the Ostspitze.

Gadin, whom I consulted by letter, in

order to verify the accuracy of my memory in several particulars, though not in that one, referred to this matter of his own accord, confirming my opinion on these three points, and concluding in his French, which I quote: " J'ai bien observé cela."

Mr. Freshfield would seem to have meant to express an opinion exactly similar to ours, when he wrote that, leaving the spot on which the stone man stood, he began the passage of the ridge leading on to the eastern peak.

After all, perhaps we should take into consideration the possible changes in level brought about at the top of Monte Rosa by the snow.

Such changes are certainly not wont to be very marked even on the highest peaks. But Mr. Freshfield speaks expressly of fresh snow on the Dufour as being so deep as to cause him to pass the stone man almost unawares.

Again, anyone who reads attentively the accounts of ascents hitherto accomplished may notice in their references, hasty and scanty though they be, like ours, to the general aspect of the ridge, a diversity of opinion among those who crossed in the same direction from the Ostspitze to the Allerhöchste.

But I am anticipating events.

Here we were on the Ostspitze, but we were unable to remain there long. Driven by the wind which, was now insufferable, and by approaching night, we soon began to descend, till we found, about thirty metres lower down, a projecting rock which was almost free from snow, and there we took up a position as best we could.

It was 8.30 p.m., and the aneroid showed a height of 4,600 metres above the sea.

The spot where we were was not indeed one of the most comfortable, and for people who had spent the day as we had, it was certainly not as good as the beds and the comforts of the Riffel. On the other hand, it was perfectly safe for anyone who was reasonably sure of himself, though it was extremely small.

It was impossible to take a step in any direction. Anyone sitting down found his feet dangling in space ; we had, however, every facility for stamping them, provided we were careful not to lose our balance. And these elementary gymnastics were most necessary.

The cold was intense ; without being able to reckon the exact degree, I may mention that our coffee was frozen hard, and our wine and our eggs resembled it, in that they were neither respectively drinkable nor eatable.

We again had recourse to our chocolate, and to a generous quantity of excellent *kirsch*, which we still had with us.

In such a place and such a temperature, it would have been the height of imprudence to allow sleep to overcome us.

But who would have slept in that pure air, which pierced our marrow, and in face of such a scene as we had before us ?

At that height . . . in the centre of the grandest of all the grand Alpine theatres . . . in that pure transparent atmosphere, under that sky of deepest blue, lit by a crescent moon and sparkling with stars as far as the eye could reach . . . in that silence . . .

Enough! I will not try to describe the indescribable. Both Professor Grasselli and I are firmly convinced that Nature is very unlikely ever to vouchsafe us a grander, a more magnificent spectacle.

We felt ourselves to be in the presence of a novel and most imposing revelation of the omnipotence and majesty of God. . . . How could we even think of the fatigue we had endured, much less complain of it?

And there are many mountaineers (I know it well, both from what I have read and what I have heard them say) who have felt in their hearts (as we did that night) the profound truth of the line which says:

" Del mondo consacrò Jeova le cime ! "

We stood there absorbed in our thoughts, when the perfect silence was broken by a sound like a mighty thunder-clap.

It was an avalanche which was breaking

loose and falling below us, but too far away to cause us any trouble.

Awestruck and amazed, we listened attentively to the terrible sound of destruction, the sight of which was denied to us, as the mass, ever increasing in volume, hurled itself downwards, with "un fracasso d' un suon pien di spavento," as Dante says, till it came to rest on the lower glacier. When silence was first restored, it seemed to us more profound and more solemn than before.

And we were to have the opportunity of enjoying from that height the spectacle, everywhere a beautiful one, of the dawn of a splendid day; we were to witness the first diffusion of light, to see the loveliest tints growing in the east, the sun appearing in splendour between the summits, and its rays spreading like a fiery mantle over a thousand peaks, and creeping down a thousand slopes of ice and snow, lighting them up with a wondrous medley of splendid tints !

It was enough to drive a painter mad . . . and for us it was time to be moving, and to climb the peak once more. The evening before we had been able to make a fairly exact estimate of the difficulties which we still had to overcome. Nevertheless, in order to move quicker and more safely, we left at the gîte the whole of our scanty baggage (the bulk of it had been sent to Zermatt by the Weissthor), taking with us nothing but the remaining axes and the ropes.

It may have been 4.45 or 5 o'clock when we left our sleeping-place, and, numb as we were, we took at least half an hour to climb up to the Ostspitze again. This peak is connected with the Dufour by a narrow ridge, the crest of which consists of frozen snow and slabs of gneiss, broken here and there by projecting rock.

Placing our feet now on one side, now on the other, at times literally straddling the ridge, and at last carefully climbing round a block and crossing a narrow and very steep gully which runs down to the Swiss Monte Rosa glacier, we found ourselves at length assembled round the stone man which stands on the Dufour peak.

It was 8.20 a.m.

The weather was still splendid, the atmosphere perfectly clear; I leave it to the reader to imagine the view from that height of over 4,600 metres, which is only surpassed by Mont Blanc, and there only by 170 metres, a difference which was rendered almost indistinguishable by the distance.

Meanwhile, however, both the cold and the wind were still with us. We swallowed a little chocolate instead of the traditional champagne, and, after putting a short report of our all-Italian ascent in a bottle which we found in a chink of the stone man, we immediately began to think of our descent.

The tracks, still perfectly plain, of the last party from Zermatt showed us the route most usually followed on the Swiss side. We were tempted to adopt it, in order to avoid returning over our ridge, which was really difficult.

But, all things considered, we thought

it better to go back to our gîte and
collect the few things we had left there,
and especially to try and recover the axe,
the lack of which was increasingly felt
by my friend.

We therefore went back along the
ridge, returned over the Ostspitze to
our gîte, took up our sacks, and then
descended (following roughly the route
taken on the ascent) by the rocks to a
point a little lower than the Zumsteinjoch
(about 4,450 metres).

Our men having failed in their attempt
to recover the lost axe, we ascended to
the Col itself, about half-way between the
Dufour and the Zumstein peaks, reaching it about 1 p.m.

Far below us lay, smooth and easy,
the Grenz or Frontier Glacier; but it
was separated from a very steep rock-
pitch by a wide crevasse, which stretched
right across as far as the eye could see,
and, resting on those rocks, there ran
right up to us one of the steepest snow
slopes I have ever seen.

Many climbers have undoubtedly

examined that wall at close quarters, and some will have climbed it in their ascent of the Dufour on its south-western side.

The strong and icy wind did not admit of our standing for a long discussion ; I was, however, very curious to see how Gadin would get us out of the difficulty. "Faites comme moi, Monsieur," he said to me ; and I saw that he began to descend backwards, with his face to the slope, making large holes in the snow with feet and hands, but taking great care first of all to dig in his axe as deeply as he could.

Readers will understand that we had to descend backwards, as on a ladder.

And we did descend, I do not know for how long, but, as it seemed to me, for a very long time.

We next passed the rock pitch, not without difficulty, working our way down and bearing somewhat to the left, where the approach to the glacier seemed rather easier. There only remained the crevasse to cross, from which we were now divided but by a moderately steep slope of good snow. We hoped in time and with patience, to find a place where the crevasse was somewhat narrower, or where there was a firm bridge across.

Gadin suggested a quicker and an equally safe plan. He first of all, and then the rest of us, moving one at a time and taking the whole length of the rope while the others stood ready to hold on if necessary, sat down on the slope just above the crevasse, first sliding and then leaping over the chasm, and so finally we found ourselves buried in the soft deep snow which covered the underlying glacier.

We had passed a place in a few minutes which might have cost us some hours.

When we reached the glacier, we felt like people setting foot at last on a broad, comfortable highway, after wandering on paths of disaster.

So we had not only descended the rocks of the Dufour peak on the Italian side, but crossed the pass which lies between the Dufour and the Zumstein peaks, a pass which would, if less difficult, be the natural route between the Monte Rosa glacier on the Italian side and the Grenz glacier on the Swiss.

The expedition accomplished by us, under the influence of the special circumstances attending it, may, as I pointed out at the outset, be of a certain importance in the mountaineering history of Monte Rosa, because ours would appear to be the first traverse of the Zumsteinjoch, which is perhaps the second highest pass in the Alps.

As regards our descent of the rocks of the Dufour peak, there can be no doubt that it was the first. I have already mentioned the forced descent by Herr Strauss and Ranggetiner from the base of those rocks downwards ; it therefore follows that Herr Strauss and we between us have accomplished the descent of the whole eastern face of Monte Rosa.

From my previous knowledge, which seems to me to be confirmed by all the Alpine writings that I have been able to consult, it would appear to be a fact that the pass had not only never been crossed, but not even reached from the Macugnaga side, and that it had only been attained (or nearly so) three times from the Zermatt side, and each time by an English party.

First of all it was reached by Messrs. F. P. Barlow and G. W. Prothero* on the 31st of August, 1874, with G. Carrel and Peter Taugwalder as guides, when they ascended the Dufour peak by this pass and along the ridge which leads from it up to the Ostspitze.

A short report of this expedition was only published four years later (February, 1878) in the *Alpine Journal*, vol. viii., No. 59, p. 400.

In the meantime, the same expedition had been repeated by others, who, indeed, believed themselves to be the first to carry it out.

On the 23rd of July, 1877, Messrs. W. M. Conway† and G. Scriven attained the pass, and from it ascended the Dufour peak, and soon gave an account of the

* The late Sir G. W. Prothero.
† Sir W. M. Conway.

climb in the *Alpine Journal* (vol. viii., No. 58, p. 338).

This brought about the publication of a notice in the following number of the *Journal*, which established the claim of Messrs. Barlow and Prothero to be considered the pioneers.

I extract from Conway's account the part which refers to the route as far as the pass.

Messrs. Conway and Scriven, with Nicholas Knubel and P. J. Truffer as guides, left the Riffel Hotel at 2.20 a.m., and went up the Grenz glacier by the ordinary route, towards the Lysjoch. At 6.30 they halted at the foot of the rocks by which the Dufour peak is usually ascended. Starting again at 7.15, they mounted that branch of the glacier which comes down from the saddle between the Dufour and Zumstein peaks, and by 8.30 they had already reached the rocks at the head of that glacier. Bearing somewhat to the left, they then climbed to the top of these rocks, and at 9 o'clock they were on the crest of the ridge, with the aforesaid saddle below them on the right.

On the 22nd of July, 1886, the same saddle was reached by Mr. W. A. B. Coolidge and Mr. Conway himself, with Chr. Almer the younger, and from it they ascended the Zumstein peak.

The account of this expedition published in vol. xiii., p. 126, of the *Alpine Journal* states that the party returned to the Riffelalp by the route already described by Messrs. Conway and Scriven.

I do not know whether any others have attained our pass by the Grenz glacier route, and, the question being now of no importance, it is quite natural that nothing more should have appeared in print about it, whereas the lack of any kind of reference to the question whether the pass has ever been climbed from the Macugnaga side bears out the supposition that we were the first to reach it from that side and to cross it.

With regard to the name to be given to the pass, the Swiss map (Siegfried) calls it the Grenz-Sattel; in the Monte

Rosa section (1 : 50,000) of Sheet 29 of the new map of the Royal Italian Institute of Military Geography it has been left unnamed, and this is not surprising, for of the few passes in the principal Monte Rosa group, the only one named and measured is the Sesiajoch, and neither the Jägerjoch, the Silber-Sattel (or Ranggetiner Pass), which is the highest in the Alps, nor even the broad, easy, and, one may say, much-frequented Lysjoch, is even named.

I need not add that our pass is not mentioned by name even on Sheet No. 29 (Monte Rosa, 1 : 100,000), which has recently been published. The same fate has attended the other passes in the group, including the Sesiajoch.

In the accounts given by the *Alpine Journal* of the three aforesaid expeditions, we see that in the first two the name of Zumstein-Sattel is adopted, whereas Conway, whose " Zermatt-Pocket-Book " (London, 1881) gives their routes, among the others, always calls it in this book the Grenz-Sattel. The report on the third ascent also uses the name of Grenz-Sattel.

In Luigi Vaccarone's "Statistics of First Ascents" (*Bollettino*, 1885, Monte Rosa group, No. 29) the name of Zumstein-Sattel is adopted; in the *Bollettino* for 1886 (*ibid.*, Nos. 26 and 105²) occurs that of Grenz-Sattel, and the same in the "Guide to the Western Alps" (Alpi Pennine), pp. 106-107, and 154-155.

I now learn that Vaccarone, being about to publish a third edition of the said "Statistics," intends to give the preference to the name of Colle Zumstein, for reasons which I consider excellent.

In the first place, this name is most suitable for our pass, because it is taken from the peak between which and the Dufour the pass lies, and because it is the name of an Italian* who was one of the first to ascend that peak.

Secondly, the name of Grenz, or

* F. Zumstein, a Piedmontese, and an inspector of forests at Gressoney, who made the first ascent of the peak with G. N. Vincent on the 12th of August, 1819.

Frontier Saddle, if it is given because the col is on the frontier ridge, does not seem any more applicable to this than to other gaps on the frontier; if it refers to the Grenz glacier, on to which one of the slopes descends from the pass, it is still less suitable, because the branch of the glacier which issues from that slope is only a secondary one; indeed, from this point of view, the name of Grenz-Sattel might much more correctly be given to the saddle between the Zumstein-Spitze and the Punta Gnifetti, from which the main stream of the Grenz glacier flows, and which, moreover, has no name at all.

Therefore, as the pass in question has been given two names, of which one is unsuitable to it, but would fit another saddle much better, whereas the other name suits the pass well, it would seem reasonable for it to retain the latter, and transfer the former where it belongs.

If we, as the first to traverse the pass, may be allowed to exercise the right to give it a name, we wish to support Vaccarone's arguments, and we propose to call it, and do call it, the Colle Zumstein.

The Grenz glacier drops for a long way in great terraces like an immense staircase; it is flanked by snowy peaks and slopes, broken at intervals by black rocks, the whole forming a noble parapet.

It was a regular desert of snow; and I recollect how those lines of Salmini's were recalled to my mind :

> " Neve, neve, sempre neve,
> Fredda, muta, fitta, lieve,
> Un altar che cava gli occhi,
> Una bianca vertigine."

Lower down, the glacier assumes the aspect and the movements of a majestic, widely winding river, and flows down to the meeting-place in the vast Gorner basin, where at least ten glaciers, coming from the Weissthor, the Nordend, the Dufour, the Twins, the Schwarzthor, the Breithorn and the Little Matterhorn, have their stately rendezvous.

In that vast theatre of lifeless nature, we felt as if we must disappear and be lost.

And the best of it was, that if we were

not exactly to be lost, we were certainly to stray from our proper path.

We knew quite well that there were paths leading by the Riffelhorn and the Gornergrat to the Riffel hotel, and Gadin knew it likewise ; but, whether his memory failed him, or whether his eyes, half-blinded by the glare of the snow, refused to render him due service in those unknown surroundings, it came about that he looked for a path where no path was.

Also, we were walking (except for the elementary precautions which are always necessary on a glacier) as people who know themselves to be near home, and see no necessity for much hurry. We halted a comfortable time at the place called Plattje, and there we were at last able to slake our thirst, which had long been tormenting us without mercy and without relief, for it is well known that snow is no remedy.

Meanwhile the sun had passed the meridian, had sunk to the west, had disappeared, and still the path failed to appear.

We passed from one glacier to the other, we climbed up the moraine to reconnoitre the rocks of the Riffelhorn at closer quarters. . . . Still no path!

Meanwhile the light was failing, and at length it grew quite dark.

We relit our one remaining lantern (the other had ended as a victim to the call of duty), but all in vain.

Anyone who knows what a great moraine is like, what a picture of chaos it presents, will have some idea of our wanderings to and fro.

In short, all our researches were fruitless, as was a reconnaissance carried out by the excellent Proment.

Only a few yards from the comfortable beds of the Riffel, we were forced to be content with passing the night on the hard stones of the moraine.

This was a small matter compared with what we had gone through, and, after all, we could well consider ourselves lucky.

During all this long time, and in such conditions as have been mentioned hitherto, we had not met with a single real danger, not one serious incident had occurred, not a foot had slipped.

Even if our present predicament could be called unfortunate, it was only right and reasonable to put a good face upon it.

Accordingly, we did so, and, choosing a place that was more comfortable and sheltered from the stones that might fall from the rocks above, we went to sleep just as the lamp refused to serve us any longer, and we slept peacefully, to the great benefit of our limbs, which by now were very well entitled to feel fatigued.

I said above "a real danger," and, in order to avoid misunderstandings, I hasten to explain the words for the benefit of those who may need explanation, and to the extent of that need.

By the words "real danger," then I mean (and we must understand the actual circumstances, because otherwise the most trifling actions and things may be called dangerous) those conditions which are presumably not to be faced with impunity either because of something inherent in themselves, or in him who goes out to meet them.

Now it would seem to us a deliberate exaggeration to speak of real dangers braved or incurred by us—that is, in our own actual case.

And as for the very real and by no means small difficulties with which we had met, I quite believe Gadin, who told me he had experienced much greater ones on other climbs.

It is clear from the respective accounts of nearly all the expeditions previous to ours, that the climbers met with dangers which were both real and serious ; but they also show plainly, if I am not mistaken, that the mountain or the weather or both, were in very different condition from what they were with us.

Undoubtedly for high mountain ascents certain external and internal or subjective conditions are indispensable (as, indeed, they are, proportionately, for everything, if it is to be done properly).

The former conditions are, if not always, at any rate in some cases, sufficiently visible and tangible to give reasonable certainty; the latter can only be obtained and adequately ensured by a graduated course of personal experience.

When they are both found together, there are few recreations which are more wholesome for body and mind, and more to be recommended, than a little mountain climbing. Clearly, the ascent of Monte Rosa by the east face is much more than " a little mountain climbing," and we thoroughly agree with our predecessors that this expedition is one that does not allow of the least lack of strength or care.

We were awakened from our deep sleep by the voice of Gadin, informing us that Proment had found the path a little above us, and that we had better go and join him at once.

We did not require telling twice, and we remounted the glacier and reached the Riffelberg.

It was time we did so; Gadin's eyes could have stood no more.

At the Riffel we enjoyed a perfect

flood of refreshing new milk, amid the curiosity and the wonder of all who were present. The curiosity and the wonder were most natural, for a report of our expedition had reached Zermatt from Macugnaga by the Weissthor, together with our baggage, and we were expected at the excellent Hôtel de la Poste.

In view of our non-appearance (the reader now knows the reasons for our delay), a telegram had been sent to the Riffel to enquire about us.

It therefore behoved us to go down to Zermatt as soon as possible, and we did so after about three-quarters of an hour's halt, leaving Gadin behind, however, so that he might pay some attention to his eyes, and then join us at his leisure.

Duty and inclination both bid me express gratitude, also on behalf of Professor Grasselli and Gadin, to the staff and guests of the hotel, and especially to an English gentleman, whose name I am sorry not to know, for their kind and beneficent treatment of our guide.

He stood greatly in need of it, and he

thoroughly deserved it, just as he deserves a final word from me, giving some expression to the satisfaction both of Professor Grasselli and myself with all he did on this expedition, and especially on the 30th of July.

I only repeat words which a famous mountaineer, Edward Whymper, once wrote about Michel Croz, one of the greatest guides in the Alps, and which seem also to fit Gadin exactly : " Could he have performed the feats upon the boards of a theatre that he did upon this occasion, he would have brought down the house with thunders of applause."*

Neither the length of our ascent, nor the varied contretemps of the descent, can persuade me that the praise I accord to Gadin is exaggerated.

Anyone who takes a comprehensive view of the separate details of my account and considers as a whole our route on the ascent, will easily see that, apart from the minor troubles we underwent, our security, which may be called absolute,

* " Scrambles," p. 260.

was purchased by increasing the length of our journey.

The continuance of the fine weather and the cold allowed us, even persuaded us, to do that which might well have been dangerous on a hot day and in weather that was not so settled.

It is well known that, as a rule, high mountain climbs should be carried out in the shortest time possible. As for the descent, experts will have realized at once that it was impossible for us to reach the endless Grenz glacier except at a very late hour.

I am not aware (I mention the fact of my ignorance, though I have examined a good many of the authorities, but I do not wish to do anyone an injustice) that anyone else has ever gone to and fro (during the same expedition) on the ridge between the Ostspitze and the Allerhöchstespitze, nor am I aware that the rocks of the Dufour peak have ever been descended by others on the Macugnaga side, nor that anyone before us had traversed the Col Zumstein.

The late hour, Gadin's trouble with his eyes, and our ignorance of the locality, are perhaps enough to explain satisfactorily why we spent a second night out almost on the threshold of the Riffel.

If we could have crossed that threshold before nightfall, it would certainly have been more comfortable and pleasanter, especially for us; but I must not say more praiseworthy, especially as regards Gadin.

His courage and skill were only equalled by his honesty and moderation when the question of payment was being discussed.

Also, we cannot but testify fully to our complete satisfaction with young Proment.

This account, such as it is, was already finished when certain foreign publications were brought to my notice, in which the difficulties and dangers of the ascent of Monte Rosa from the Macugnaga side are discussed.

The names of famous mountaineers and Alpine writers, both English and German, occur in the discussions; the

H

most recent of these publications, as far as I know, date from the beginning of 1889.

Herr Schulz, in the account he gave of his climb, was charged with being dangerously optimistic, so that he might easily have brought about rash attempts and deplorable catastrophes.

Herr Schulz defended himself from the accusation, but admitted that he had not emphasized sufficiently the difficulties of the expedition. For the benefit of anyone who wishes to learn more about the matter, I quote here the principal journals which deal with it.

We are glad to know about these difficulties now, but more fortunate in not realising them before our expedition.

Our judgment of the condition of the weather and the mountain, on which our ascent must depend, was the calmer and the more objective in proportion to its freedom from bias ; and, at any rate, we cannot accuse Professor Schulz's optimism, with which he was perhaps rather unjustly charged, of having seduced us unawares.

I say " perhaps rather unjustly charged," because there is possibly a little pessimism in the accusation.

Naturally, I do not say this because it was on Professor Schulz's motion that the Leipzig section of D.Oe.A.V. refused to contribute to the cost of building the Marinelli hut, which he disapproved.

It was Professor Schulz himself who said it in No. 3 of the 1889 *Mittheilungen*, which I have quoted several times. In any case, as regards his personal opinion and judgment, Professor Schulz was the more unbiassed in that he had not been able to make use of the hut, because it was not begun till two years after his ascent of the Dufour peak.

I have said all this because it seems to me to follow from Herr Schulz's defence, which was not only spirited, but straightforward and generous.

Even too generous, I think ; as, for instance, where he concludes that, instead of " under no circumstances whatever " (" under no circumstances, however favourable " ; this was the formula in which Professor Bonney deprecated any fresh attempt to ascend the Dufour from Macugnaga, and in which Signor Kugy concurred) he would say: "Not as a rule; but only under specially favourable circumstances, which cannot be reckoned on with sufficient certainty and knowledge, and concerning which it is difficult to form a reasonably sure judgment, and almost impossible (generally speaking) to attain to an infallible one."

As regards ourselves, at any rate, we are convinced that we were never exposed to any real danger, and that we were right to be sufficiently confident and sure that such would be the case even before we started on the climb.

In the case of such expeditions as this, I admit that it is never easy to attain to such certainty beforehand, and that it is much more difficult with regard to the east face of Monte Rosa than for other mountains.

But I could not deny the possibility altogether, without being contradicted by the facts.

Gadin is entitled to all the credit of having seen and realised with clear, unerring insight the true conditions existing at the time.

And, if I mistake not, this insight, which I may call one of time and place, which is inseparable, but quite distinct, from the general conclusions which experience alone can supply, is one of the most valuable and most indispensable qualities of a guide.

I have never seen this quality so conspicuous as in Gadin ; I could therefore feel no surprise when I read of the ascent of Mont Blanc by a new route (or at any rate a route followed in its entirety for the first time) as having been successfully accomplished by the members of the Turin section, with him and Petigax as guides, a few days after our expedition.

Moreover, it is thanks to this quality of his that we on our ascent took without hesitation a route which was certainly longer, but, in my opinion, undoubtedly safer, than those of our predecessors.

I have again mentioned the Marinelli hut. . . .

I was aware of the opposition it had met with abroad, even during its embryonic stage; this opposition had been replied to briefly but most convincingly by the translator of Zsigmondy's account (Count Lurani), himself a well-known mountaineer.

It is only now, however, that I have learnt that the poor hut drew down upon the Milan section the same accusation, or nearly so, which befell Herr Schulz, and it seems to me that after enjoying the hospitality of the accused, it would be neither generous nor grateful on my part if I said nothing about the matter.

After Count Lurani's remarks, and the experiences of ourselves and others, in view of the ease and the ample attractions even of an expedition going no further than the hut (these attractions are mentioned in the Milan section's circular of the 14th of January, 1885), it seems to me impossible that any suspicion can be expressed—even hypothetically—as to the

Milan section having built the hut merely for the sake of encouraging repetitions of a dangerous enterprise ; such a purpose would be most blameworthy, if it existed.

The above-mentioned circular does, certainly, speak of the ascent of the Dufour peak being made easier, and of all danger being set aside, by means of the Marinelli hut ; and it may be admitted that such language may seem bold.

But, after all, I can see no harm in it.

No mountaineer, even if only just initiated into Alpine climbing and literature, could possibly be for a single moment in doubt as to the real meaning of such language, especially as intended by its author.

Moreover, I repeat that I do not think it possible to deny categorically that all danger may be eliminated in certain circumstances, however rare and however improbable they may be said to be.

Given such circumstances, which are naturally assumed to be present, it would have been quite legitimate to say that the hut facilitates the ascent and contributes to the elimination of the danger, in that it enables the climber to take advantage of those very circumstances promptly and with freshly renewed strength.

Anyhow, whatever may be said or thought of the language in question, it obviously was not, and never will be, able to make the hut itself more of an encouragement than it is in reality.

Anyone who walks up to the Pedriolo Alp, and from there carefully examines the east face of Monte Rosa, will understand at once, even without going into the cemetery at Macugnaga, that it is not on the hut that a reasonable hope of a successful ascent of the Dufour peak can be based; that many other factors quite foreign to the hut, and independent of it, require consideration and decide the question of success or failure; and that, with regard to that question, the hut can only offer the advantage mentioned above, which, though limited, is not insignificant.

No, I am wrong: this poor hut of the Milan section can render a much more valuable service, which the section that built it was neither under the necessity nor the obligation of pointing out.

The hut, standing at a convenient and perfectly safe point of vantage near the tracks of the avalanches, enables the climber to watch his enemy at close quarters, and, if he should hear him stirring in the night, even if it be only in the neighbourhood of the dreaded couloir, to beat a safe and easy retreat, which would be, under those conditions, not only honourable, but wise, and, as I think, a matter of duty.

We, as we have told each other in so many words, would certainly not have refused such an honour, however modest it might be.

After all, if there is any need to say so once more, the intention here has been to give an account, accurate if possible, but certainly honest, of a particular concrete case, and not to establish general rules or to give encouragement of any kind to any person.

I am far from attaching to our expedition any importance other or greater than the relative one which it may receive from the goodwill of lovers of the high mountains. I thank God for that He has allowed me to admire at close quarters beauties which are certainly amongst the greatest and the grandest in this visible world He has created. I am glad that we have been the means of filling no inconsiderable gap in the history of the Club Alpino Italiano ; and I venture to hope that others may meet with such a concatenation of favourable circumstances that they may enjoy similar and even greater pleasure, not only in equal security, but also, if it be possible, as I believe it is, with fewer discomforts and difficulties.

Difficulties and discomforts, if faced under suitable conditions, and with the requisite precautions, disappear, leaving body and mind refreshed and strengthened, with an imperishable memory of those great and marvellous scenes,

" che di vederli in me stesso m' esalto."*

* Dante, *Inferno*, iv., 130.

CHAPTER FOUR

ASCENT OF THE MATTERHORN DIRECT FROM ZERMATT*

I HAD arrived at Zermatt on the 1st of August, 1889, with Professor Grasselli, after traversing (with him) Monte Rosa from Macugnaga over the Dufour peak, together with Giuseppe Gadin and Alessio Proment of Courmayeur.

If I proceed once more to bore the readers of our journals, it is entirely the fault of my good friend the editor, who says that unreported expeditions are on the consciences of the members responsible.

The 2nd, as will be readily believed, was a day of rest; on the 3rd, I began

* From the *Rivista Mensile* of the Italian Alpine Club, February, 1890, vol. ix., No. 2, pp. 65-68.

to be sensible of the presence of the Matterhorn, which is at Zermatt a real "influence." I made a reconnaissance almost as far as the new hut, and I enjoyed, in magnificent weather, the view from the Hörnli.

The 4th was a Sunday, and was again a rest day, properly celebrated by the good Valaisans and a good many of the visitors to Zermatt.

About sunset, on my return from an easy walk, I ran into Francesco Bich of Valtournanche, a famous Matterhorn guide. It was soon agreed that he should accompany me on the climb, together with Gadin and Proment, to whom, as to me, it was quite new.

We started on the morning of the 5th, and at dawn we were at the Schwarzsee Hotel, a dependance of the Hôtel de la Poste, at which we were stopping, and situated two hours' walk above the village.

But the weather was changing for the worse, though not sufficiently to prevent the characteristic *festa* of our Lady of the

Snows, which it is customary to celebrate, amid a great concourse of clergy and people, in the lonely chapel near the hotel, at the edge of the lake.

I regret that I have no space or time to describe it, but if anyone else likes to betake himself to that spot on the 5th of August, he may be quite certain of enjoying a very fine sight.

Weather conditions inclining to improve in the afternoon, I spent the night at the Schwarzsee, but in vain, for on the morning of the 6th it was blowing hard, and the sky promised anything but good weather. About 3 p.m. we reluctantly decided to return to Zermatt . . . with our tails between our legs.

And behold, half-way down, we met one, two, three parties, on their way towards the Matterhorn with provisions for passing the night in the hut.

We argued that down in the valley they must have had some indication of approaching fine weather which had not yet become apparent in the upper regions.

I descended farther, and a cool, dry

breeze, blowing up towards the heights, assured us of the truth. Our first thought was to return to the Schwarzsee, but we were too near the village; we decided, however, that if the favourable symptoms continued, we would start again for the Matterhorn at midnight, going straight on to the summit without stopping the night at the hut.

It was an experiment of some interest: and, at any rate, we should, if successful, have done the climb in our own way, and that an uncommon one.

By 2 a.m. on the 7th we were once more at the Schwarzsee; by 4.15 we had reached the new hut, having lost some little time on the way, owing to the darkness.

The parties we had met the previous evening had left the hut some time before. When we consider that, reckoning travellers and guides, they consisted of twenty people or thereabouts, it will be readily understood that we had not lost much by not sleeping up there. We stopped at the hut for rather less than half an hour, in order to eat something and then we started up by the ordinary route.

We went from rock to rock, from ridge to ridge, from rope to rope, till, somewhat below the so-called shoulder, we met the other parties already on their way down.

We were warned by their guides that the snow up above was not in good condition, and that in some places even the rocks were slightly coated with it.

The delay inseparable from the circumstances attending our expedition (I do not mention this with a view to describing our route) had already led us confidently to anticipate trouble up above and we were now more than ever convinced of it; but where so many people had ascended and returned without any untoward incident, we thought we might well venture to go on.

If there ever was a day on which it was justifiable to take a risk, it was this one, so fine and promising was the weather.

So we continued on our upward way but we strictly put into practice what

Whymper wrote in his description of his first tragic ascent : " The work became difficult and required caution."

We had reached the very spot to which Whymper referred in the sentence I have quoted.

As seen from Zermatt, it looks quite inaccessible : it is not really so, but it is only practicable for those who can depend absolutely on their sure-footedness and on the strength of their arms, especially in such conditions of the snow.

At last, about 4 or 4.30 p.m., we were on the top. The sun, sinking to its rest, was spreading its final splendour over the magnificent, indescribable scene. I shall never forget the awful beauty of the precipices which fall vertically from the summit on the Valtournanche side.

We saw at once that the snow and the verglas made an ascent from that side impossible for the time being.

But meanwhile the sun was sinking steadily, and an icy wind made us think of our descent.

Bich, who had hurt his foot, probably

in some violent effort on the highest rocks, surrendered the first place to Gadin, behind whom I was placed.

We had only descended a short distance, when we became aware that the snow itself was beginning to feel the cold : it was getting coated with a kind of varnish of ice.

The need for discipline and care became ever more urgent : speed in the descent, for which the lateness of the hour seemed to call, must necessarily be sacrificed to security.

But on snow and ice Gadin was always in his element.

Only one of us moved at a time ; in the most difficult places, when he thought I was firmly placed, Gadin merely told me to hold the rope taut, and I could see him below me, upright on the precipice, and swinging his axe with a skill and an accuracy which did not lack an element of grace.

Someone once asked me what would have happened if Gadin had by some accident fallen.

I replied that, if such a supposition could have presented itself seriously to anyone, it would have done so to me, but that it never did, or could, occur to me, knowing and seeing as I did how well Gadin worked.

But, after all, I verily believe that, with our method of procedure, I could have held him unaided, as I had for several minutes held my companion (no light weight) on the Gran Paradiso, two years before (in 1887), when before my eyes he fell off the topmost ridge on the side of the Glacier de la Tribulation.

We had for a short time hoped to reach, by some means or other, the old hut before dark, and to spend the night there.

It was not to be, however, and not far below the shoulder we decided that it would be best to stop.

The weather was still perfect, and we resigned ourselves to passing the night where we were, not only without regret, but, I venture to say, with considerable enjoyment.

The singular form of the Matterhorn,

the perfect isolation in which its gigantic peak is thrust up through the air to heaven, the varied aspect of the country at its foot, made that night seem to me in some ways even more wonderful than the one I had spent a week before quite near the top of Monte Rosa.

We were all of us in the best of spirits. My men, Bich especially, were full of song, and their powerful voices, resounding in the lofty silence of that sublime solitude, gave me a most delightful impression.

The cold was intense, and, though we did not fail to clap our hands and stamp our feet, we felt that we should not be able to resume our descent until the sun had risen and restored our elasticity and strength.

At our leisure, therefore, we watched him rise and climb up into the sky, and then we made our way down to the old hut, and thence, after a short halt, to the new, where we lit a fire and refreshed ourselves in comfort.

On arriving at the Hörnli, I was agreeably surprised to see Professor Grasselli, who had come up so far by himself to meet me.

At about 1.30 p.m. we were at the Schwarzsee Hotel; a couple of hours later we started and descended quickly to Zermatt, where we were awaited for a farewell dinner by the good parish priest, a learned and zealous Churchman, revered by his flock and esteemed by the visitors, who easily made friends with him by reason of his knowledge of several languages and his charming manner. He was a true type of the mountaineer, both in body and mind, and a really good climber.

I will forgive the editor his exactions because he has given me the opportunity of mentioning my good host and friend, and of thanking him publicly for all his kindness and courtesy.

I had found Bich a cheerful travelling companion and an excellent rock climber. It is not necessary for me to say any more in his praise, beyond quoting a remark he made to me about Gadin, which sufficiently proves his goodness of heart. He said, alluding especially to the first part of the descent: "Gadin is a very good man."

I have said all I have to say when I relate that on the next day, Friday, the 9th of August, we reached Valtour-nanche, two hours before nightfall, after fair halts at the so-called Forni and at Breuil. On Saturday, the 10th, we descended joyfully and swiftly to Châtillon, and by 5.30 p.m., on the same day, we were treading the pavements of Milan.

I had long wished to enjoy the spectacle of twilight and night in the high mountains. My desire was fully satisfied this year.

My few expeditions prove once more that, given good conditions of weather, and, I may add, of body and mind, it is possible to spend the night out with impunity at the greatest heights in the Alps.

The indescribable beauty of the surroundings, and the assured possibility of priceless experiences, which can only be enjoyed during a somewhat lengthy sojourn on the highest peaks, and then only at hours when one is least wont to be there, lead me to welcome most heartily the new hut—highest of all huts—which the C.A.I. is preparing to build on the Punta Gnifetti.

CHAPTER FIVE

MONT BLANC: ASCENT BY THE ROCHER
ROUTE AND DESCENT BY THE DÔME
GLACIER*

ON the evening of the 27th of July,
1890, Professor Grasselli and I were
at Courmayeur, having travelled thither
from Milan as the crow flies, I may say.

We wished to avenge ourselves for our
failure on Mont Blanc two years before;
and, in order that our revenge might be
complete, we intended to attempt the
descent to Courmayeur by the route that
was first discovered and used on the
ascent by Cav. A. E. Martelli and his
friends of the Turin section, on the 16th
and 17th of August, 1889.

Giuseppe Gadin and Alessio Proment,

* From the *Rivista Mensile* of the Italian Alpine
Club, September, 1890, vol. ix., No. 9, pp. 326-330.

our old friends and guides, were expecting us. Gadin, who, with Petigax, also of Courmayeur, had guided the above expedition, was not only thoroughly favourable to our plan, but hoped (I must say now " believed," as I believed it till some weeks afterwards) that he could add to it a greater and more complete novelty, as will be seen from the short tale I have to tell.

On the 28th and 29th we took two fine training walks—the first up the Crammont on the Courmayeur side, the second to the Col du Géant.

The second walk, which was made more interesting by the great quantity of snow, proved even more delightful to us on account of our meeting at the hut with that great mountaineer Avv. G. Bobba of Turin, who is now well known to all those who have read the last *Bollettino* of the C.A.I.

Who would have thought that that spot, which proved so delightful and so hospitable to us, was only a few days later to be fatal to the poor guide Brunod, and that this catastrophe was to be the prelude to a season memorable for disaster in the annals of the C.A.I., a season which deprived the club of a popular member and of some of its best guides?

At about 8 o'clock on the morning of the 30th, we set out on our way to the Rocher du Mont Blanc and the Sella hut, in weather that was fine and promised to become finer still.

Our party had received the welcome addition of the Rev. Giovanni Bonin, curate of Pré St. Didier, a vigorous native of the Val d' Aosta. Gadin assured us that he was as good as a guide, and the event proved him right.

We walked up at an easy pace, thinking thus to continue our brief training, and by 4 p.m. we were at the hut.

We had been preceded thither by Signor Carones, a fellow-member of the Milan section, with his guides, Petigax and Croux of Courmayeur, and we spent a joyous evening with them.

On the morning of the 31st the weather was splendid, and the mountain looked

magical in the moonlight. Signor Carones started at 3 a.m., and we at 4. We
caught him up on the rocks, and by noon
we had all reached the summit by the
ordinary route. Some sparkling Asti,
quite priceless in that place, proved an
excellent substitute for champagne.

Not a single cloud had marred our view
of the most wonderful panoramas on our
brief halts during the ascent.

When we reached the summit, the sky
was still fairly clear on the French side,
but on the Italian there had arisen a sea
of mist which came up to within a few
hundred metres of the summit. Our
peak, and a number of lesser ones, stood
out above the mist like islands, piercing
the pure clear sky above with their
bristling rocky precipices and their glitter-
ing ice and snow.

There was no wind, no trace of cold :
it was even rather warm—" A little too
warm," said Gadin.

And it was precisely the warmth, rather
than the mist, which turned us from our
purpose of attempting the descent to

Courmayeur on the same day. This descent by snowy ridges and glaciers would have been a rash undertaking, hardly admissible, even if successful.

Moreover, we had foreseen the contingency and had decided, if it should occur, to ask hospitality of the builders of the Vallot Observatory Refuge, whom we knew to be encamped underneath the Bosses.

Gadin was aware also that the hut was nearly finished, and that we should probably be able to pass the night there.

And so it turned out : we left the top at 2 p.m., and by 3.30 we were at the hut.

They were just giving the finishing touches, and M. Vallot was expected there with his wife on the following day.

This hut is known to be, for the present, the highest in the Alps (about 4,460 metres). I say "for the present," because it will be surpassed by the Observatory Refuge which the C.A.I. is about to build on the Punta Gnifetti at 4,559 metres.

Signor Carones intended to descend to

Chamonix by the Grands Mulets. We spent the night at the hut (this, too, was something of a novelty), and, as far as I was concerned, a very good night too.

I have read in some description of an ascent of Mont Blanc that it is impossible to sleep in high Alpine huts on a great climb. During that night I slept seven good hours without a break; the night before, in the Sella hut, I had slept much less, because Gadin had been obliged to wake me much earlier.

I will not take up time in giving a minute description of the Observatory Refuge, especially as the Alpine journals have already dealt with it, and will do so again in the future.

It is (or at least it was when we were there) a small, very strong and very well-built construction of wood founded on rock, facing the snowy field or plateau which stretches between the Bosses and the Dôme du Goûter.

As measured by eye, I thought its area was about $2\frac{1}{2}$ metres square, and its height about the same or a little more at the top—that is, at the angle formed by the junction of the two sides of the roof.

The interior, which is lighted by two small windows, has its capacity almost doubled by a floor which divides it at a height of little more than a metre from the ground. This explains how we, and others besides us, eight persons in all, were able to find room and to pass the night in the hut. What I cannot understand is what I read after my return in some paper, which described the Bosses hut as a capacious building with three rooms, consisting of the observatory, the kitchen, and the dormitory, the latter capable of accommodating I don't know how many dozen beds.

The Vallot hut, as we saw it and appreciated it, is admirable enough, without its being necessary to spread abroad incredible tales about it.

When I saw those workmen labouring in their hairy caps, their dark spectacles, their thick gloves and their enormous heavy boots, amid that immense theatre of snow and ice, I really thought I was reading an illustrated description of a polar expedition.

I only fulfil a duty in recording the tact, the civility, the true cordiality with which we were welcomed and treated, thanks especially to a Payot, one of the excellent and well-known Chamonix guides of that name, and the leader in the work.

We left the lofty and hospitable hut at 6 a.m. on the 1st of August, climbed up the Dôme du Goûter, keeping to the ridge, along which we proceeded for a short distance astride, and then descended to a point not far above the Col de Bionnassay, which lay before us, on our right.

Here, had we followed the route taken on their ascent by our fellow-members of the Turin section, we should, if I am not mistaken, have gone on to the cliffs and buttresses of the Aiguille Grise, which rise above the head of the upper Miage glacier, have crossed the glacier itself to its right bank, descended thence to a point under the Col de Miage, and then gone down by the glacier of that name.

The route lay quite clearly before us.

The explorers of August, 1889, had pointed out that the only difficulty, but a very real one, lay in the séracs of the icefall with which we should have had to deal after crossing the glacier, a difficulty not free from danger, owing to the continual threat from above.

It is true that for us, thanks to the early hour (it was 8 a.m.), only the difficulty remained, without the danger.

But a passage under séracs is always, and at all hours, to be avoided, if possible, especially on the Italian side of Mont Blanc, which is not generally very cold, on account of its favourable position.

This consideration led us most willingly to agree to the alternative suggested by Gadin, which I had mentioned at the very beginning, and which we now proceeded to attempt.

Instead of going on to the cliffs and buttresses of the Aiguille Grise, we turned at right angles to our left, and began to descend from its very beginning the Glacier du Dôme—the glacier, that is, which runs down between the Rocher du Mont Blanc on the left and the Aiguille Grise on the right.

I had found the name of Glacier du Dôme applied to it by Durier in the topographical map attached to his splendid book on Mont Blanc, which indicates the routes followed on the various ascents down to 1880.

I cannot, however, find any name assigned to our glacier in the other topographical maps, including those of Mieulet and Viollet-le-Duc, or even the new Italian map.

Though very steep at its head, and very much crevassed lower down, the Glacier du Dôme is no more difficult than many others which are much frequented. Nevertheless, I hardly think it would be wise, even if it were possible, to try and follow it down to its foot, or, rather, to its mouth, where it joins the lower Miage glacier.

Therefore, after descending for a couple

of hours, keeping to the centre of the glacier, at about 10 a.m. we turned again at a right angle to its right bank, where we reached the rocks without difficulty and clambered up on to the crest of the spur which supports the final peak of the Aiguille Grise.

Gadin said he was sure of being able to descend on to the Glacier de Miage by the other side of this spur.

We were obliged to spend some time in looking for a possible route, but we found one at last, slightly above the lowest precipices of the spur, which were quite impracticable, and here we met once more with the first signs of grass, a pleasant sight after the white monotony of ice and snow.

By about 12.30 we were on the Glacier de Miage; and a short half-hour after that, where the glacier begins to be covered with loose matter, we halted, had something to eat, and drank our fill of water. By 5 p.m. we were at the Hôtel Mont Blanc at Courmayeur.

If it be remembered that at 6 a.m. we

I

were still at the Vallot hut, and allowance be made for the precautions and the uncertainties which are inseparable from new routes (or routes new to the party concerned) in the High Alps, our route may perhaps be thought worthy of attention, especially as we are unable to point to any part of it as being, I do not say dangerous, but even really difficult or out of the ordinary.

The reader will certainly have noticed that no mention has been made of our route as a new one, save as one which we believed in good faith to be new.

My good faith—I should have said my ignorance—received an opportune shock and enlightenment from the author of the "Statistics of First Ascents." There is nothing further to be said; he is quite right, and he is quite the proper person to point out that our route had already been followed, likewise on the descent, by Messrs. Macdonald, Grove, and Buxton on the 7th of August, 1865, with Jacob Anderegg, P. Cachat, and the younger Taugwald as guides.

Mr. Macdonald wrote a full description of the expedition in the *Alpine Journal* (vol. ii., pp. 332-341), and a short extract was made by Durier (vol. ii., pp. 328-329), who apparently intended, in the map mentioned above, to indicate the route followed by the three Englishmen.

I say "intended," because the line shown by Durier seems to me very different from that referred to by Macdonald (vol. ii., p. 335, note).

According to the latter's account, he and his party descended the eastern branch of the two into which the upper Glacier du Dôme is divided; whereas Durier's plan mentions the western branch— namely, the one we took. It is perhaps worth while making this slight correction.

Besides justifying in part our claim to a new descent, it replaces in their natural position the "incredible difficulties" mentioned and portrayed (and, perhaps, somewhat accentuated in the fearsome illustration in the *Alpine Journal*, vol. ii.) by Macdonald, and changed over by

Durier in his map from one branch to the other of the Glacier du Dôme ; for, I repeat, the branch we used, which is precisely the one indicated by Durier, confronted us with no difficulty out of the common.

It was only by losing their way in the bad atmospheric conditions that the three Englishmen came down the eastern branch of the Glacier du Dôme, and took twenty-four hours to reach the Glacier de Miage, while they had intended to descend by the route taken on their ascent by Messrs. Adams-Reilly and Birkbeck, who had left St. Gervais the year before, and had climbed the Dôme du Goûter via the Col de Miage.

Gadin, who was most competently seconded by Proment, only strengthened the excellent opinion we had formed of him on our former expeditions.

On the following morning we started via Aosta for Milan, while Gadin again climbed by the Rocher du Mont Blanc the highest peak in the Alps, acting as guide to the daring, and now famous,

" armed ascent," which also adopted our route on the descent.*

* On the 3rd of August, 1890, Mont Blanc was ascended and descended by the same route as Drs. Ratti and Grasselli's by a fully armed and equipped party of the 4th Alpini, consisting of five officers and six other ranks.

CHAPTER SIX

A MISADVENTURE WHICH BEFELL PRINCE E. GONZAGA OF MILAN AND HIS GUIDE, GIUSEPPE GADIN OF COURMAYEUR, IN THE VAL BELVISO*

GIUSEPPE GADIN, the well-known guide of Courmayeur, was at Milan on private business of his own, when he was requested by Prince E. Gonzaga of the Milan section to accompany him on the traverse from Bondione (in the Val Seriana) to the Valtelline.

They left Milan on the 30th of March last, and reached Bondione late the same night.

At 2.30 a.m. on the 31st, they left the village and walked up the valley on the

* From the *Rivista Mensile* of the Italian Alpine Club, April, 1891, vol. x., No. 4, pp. 127-128.

left bank of the Serio. They intended to make their way up to the Piano di Barbellino, and thence to reach the pass by the Val Morta and to descend to Chiuso.

It was most unfortunate that the mutual confidence engendered by the magnificent strength of the prince and the well-known skill of Gadin induced them to set aside the latter's suggestion as to the advisability of enlisting the services of a local man, in view especially of the quantity of fresh snow on the mountain.

At sunrise they reached the top of the rock bastion down which leaps the great fall of the Serio. Under the conditions then existing they had a long, difficult, and wearisome ascent by an icy couloir, till they found themselves a few steps from the Barbellino hut (belonging to the Bergamo section).

From this point they were able to realize the enormous quantities of snow covering the plateau and the surrounding peaks.

But, though further progress seemed

difficult, the descent by two men only, roped though they were, appeared to be very imprudent.

Soon after a snowstorm came on. Even at Milan the morning of the 31st was cold and wet and windy.

Driven by the storm and bewildered by the clouds of snow it raised, they began to make their way up towards the Piano di Barbellino, thinking that this would lead them in the direction of their proposed destination. Instinct, it would seem, caused them to take the route that appeared to be the most open, the least in shadow, and the most practicable.

They ate a hasty mouthful about 10 a.m., and, their only anxiety being to advance as quickly as possible, in face of the serious hindrance of the snow and the storm, they kept on their way right up to the Barbellino lake.

This they found iced over, and so deeply covered with snow, that they would not have noticed it had it not been for the smoothness of its surface and shores.

It was near sunset when the broad saddle lying between the Pizzo Torrena and the Pizzo Strinato became visible to my weary and bewildered friends.

Gadin, seeing the approach of night, proposed to go on alone, as quickly as possible, in order to cast his eye over the country lying on the other side of the pass, and, taking advantage of the last of the daylight, to form some idea of its nature. His plan showed foresight, and may have saved two lives.

When they were once more united on the pass, they could be in no doubt either as to what they must do or as to their direction. To stop where they were meant death; it was necessary for them to reach the bottom of the Belviso valley, which in its lower part is called the Valle di Pila, and, turning to the left, to keep on constantly down that valley.

And down they went—down all through the night, in complete darkness, ever on the snow, which was now icy, now powdery, now soft, ever careful not to lose one another, trying to avoid and to overcome as best they could the steep pitches of rock, ever on the alert not to slip, and not to be buried in the snow-drifts. In a word, it was a long and desperate struggle against the death that threatened them from so many sides.

The remembrance of this is the only clear impression that remains to the two who so narrowly escaped destruction. After about an hour's descent, the prince dropped his stick, and it was impossible to find it again in such darkness. Gadin handed him over his axe, which was destined lower down, though it broke in two, to check, though it could not prevent, a short fall.

When the sun rose once more, they were within sight of Tresenda, and it was only then, when the struggle for life was somewhat relaxed, that the prince's powers refused all further effort, though his endurance and courage had inspired Gadin with the greatest admiration.

Assistance was promptly afforded him, and he reached the village, but quite a superficial examination sufficed to convince them both of the serious and distressing realities of the position.

The prince's feet and the guide's right hand, to mention only the principal damage, were severely frost-bitten, and required immediate remedies.

Gadin, having called in the excellent local doctor, Signor Morelli, and having helped the prince to bed, started in a carriage for Ponte Valtellina, whence he sent a telegram to Milan.

On the following day, as he felt that his previous engagements required his presence, he proceeded thither himself, but not before he had returned to the prince, and seen for himself how the treatment was progressing.

This treatment was prescribed and carried out with so much zeal and skill by the above-mentioned Signor Morelli and our worthy young friend Dr. Sormani, that it enabled the prince to be brought to Milan no later than the 15th of April with the certainty of a complete, if not an early, recovery.

It may not be without interest to

mountaineers to learn the principal points of this treatment, which can be summed up in very few words : alternate massage with snow and compresses of spirits of camphor, followed by bandaging with cotton-wool and india-rubber, which latter, on Dr. Sormani's suggestion, was applied directly to the affected parts with immediate benefit.

Another form of treatment which is often adopted by doctors in Alpine centres, and which is usually successful, was seen by the writer to effect a complete cure two years ago in the case of a friend of his, though it was applied after two days' delay, and though the patient's condition was evidently much more serious than that of Gadin in the present instance. This treatment consists of continual compresses of spirits of camphor, supplemented by vaseline and baths of cold salt water.

Just two more observations, and I have done.

Some have wondered at so grave a case of frost-bite in the foot-hills ; but similar cases have occurred even on the humblest of the Brianza hills. Moreover, it is sufficiently explained by my friends' long exposure to the snow and wind, which always bring in their train great falls in temperature.

The surprise of others at the loss of direction may seem to have more basis.

But, if wind and clouds of snow may be considered as at least equivalent to mist, there have been many cases more surprising still : Whymper, one of the boldest and best of mountaineers, with such guides as Croz and Almer, was caught by the mist while crossing the Col d' Hérens, and lost his way more than once, notwithstanding his determined efforts to keep in the right direction. Again, in 1865, three English climbers with first-class guides came down to Courmayeur on the Italian side of Mont Blanc, though they had intended (and indeed, believed themselves to be) descending on the French side to St. Gervais. Almost every winter at Milan, when the fog is thick, there are people who lose their way in streets whose every pebble is known to them. This being admitted, the aid of a local man would always have been a valuable precaution, but it is difficult to say how far it would have helped them, except by ensuring their return by the rocks of the waterfall.

After all, while my friends' mishap is only too rich in warnings for mountain climbers ; while the latter are enabled at the cost of the former to learn once more the necessity of certain precautions, to exercise a wider foresight in view of the events we have related, my friends themselves may congratulate themselves and thank Heaven that, having become honestly engaged in a truly formidable contest, they fought the fight valiantly, and came out of it wounded, it is true— a small matter for those who have contended for many hours hand to hand with death—but victorious.

Printed and Made in Great Britain by The Crypt House Press, Limited, Gloucester and London